Not Mad, Most Noble Festus

Essays on the Renewal Movement

David Parry, OSB

NOT MAD, MOST NOBLE FESTUS

Essays on the Renewal Movement

Darton, Longman & Todd Ltd

First published in Great Britain in 1979
by Darton, Longman & Todd Ltd
89 Lillie Road, London SW6 1UD

© 1979 David Parry OSB

ISBN   0   232   51442   9

Printed in Great Britain by the Anchor Press Ltd
and bound by Wm Brendon & Son Ltd,
both of Tiptree, Essex

Contents

Acknowledgements

The author wishes to offer his thanks to the Rev. James Hawes, and the Rev. G. Marsden, S. J., for reading the manuscript, and to the Rev. Benedict Heron O.S.B. and many others for help in gathering materials for this book.

D.J.P.

Whereupon, O King Agrippa, I was not disobedient unto the heavenly vision: . . . Having therefore obtained help of God, I continue unto this day, witnessing both to small and great, saying none other things than those which the prophets and Moses did say should come: That Christ should suffer and that he should be the first that should rise from the dead, and should shew light unto the people and to the Gentiles. And as he spake thus for himself, Festus said with a loud voice, Paul thou art beside thyself; much learning doth make thee mad. But he said, I am not mad, most noble Festus; but speak forth words of truth and soberness. (Acts 26.19, 22–5, Authorised Version)

The Roman Governor Festus, as a practical man recognised that Paul was not a criminal, nor a political agitator. What then was this desperate quarrel all about? It was something to do with the Jewish religion, in which King Agrippa was reckoned an expert. So as a matter of interest Paul was granted a hearing before the governor and the King. . . .

And as with shining eyes and outstretched hands Paul grew enthusiastic as he came to proclaim that Christ was risen from the dead, the first of many resurrections, a light dawned on Festus. Unfortunately it was the wrong light. 'Paul,' he said, 'you are mad.' And even as his brother Peter some years before had protested 'We are not drunk' so Paul replied, 'I am not mad. I am speaking nothing but sober truth.'

And in a way something similar still comes up for judgement. When enthusiasm for the Gospel fills ordinary men and women, putting a new light in their eyes, or altering the pattern of their speech or of their lives, is it a sign that they have gone a little mad or that they cannot disobey the heavenly vision, in however modest a form it came to them, setting them to bear witness to great and small alike?

———

1   This Charismatic Thing

The present Charismatic Movement in the Catholic Church is usually considered to draw its origin from a visit made in 1967 by Catholics of Notre Dame University, Pittsburgh to the prayer-meetings of their Pentecostal friends. They were not led by curiosity, but by a sense of non-satisfaction with their existing spiritual programmes, and as so many others, by a feeling of searching for something deeper and more satisfying. Future investigations may well show that the origins of the widespread movement of spiritual renewal in the Catholic Church were in fact more diverse than this. But certainly from the American source has spread a current of spiritual force which has rapidly passed into all parts of the Catholic world, overtaking in the speed of its growth similar movements which had been making inroads into other Churches for some time before.

The original seekers claimed to have 'received the Spirit' from their experience, and to find that they could be instruments in passing on what they had received. From an orthodox Catholic point of view this was a highly suspicious beginning, and not from the point of view of orthodox Catholics only. For in general the Pentecostals had a bad image in the United States. In fact when the sociologist, Fr Killian McDonnell O.S.B., set out to evaluate the movement in 1970, he found that his first problem was that 'The public image of Pentecostalism is so bad, that Pentecostals hardly ever receive a fair hearing.'[1]

---

[1] Fr Killian McDonnell, *Catholic Pentecostalism: Problems in Evaluation* (1970) p. 4.

According to him: 'Pentecostalism conjures up images of emotionalism, fanaticism, religious mania, illiteracy, anti-intellectualism, credulity, messianic postures and panting after miracles.'

He goes on to state that although the history of Pentecostalism contains 'bizarre aspects', yet today:

> For vast areas of the Pentecostal world, there is a basic falsity about the public image. In these areas the public image has the same relationship to the essential quality and witness of Pentecostalism as the Inquisition, the massacre of S. Bartholomew's Day, and Alexander VI have to do with the essential quality and witness of Roman Catholicism. In fact these belong to Catholic history, and are bearers of a historical truth, but do not we hope, image forth the inner reality of Roman Catholicism.

If Fr McDonnell had been writing for an English public rather than an American one, he might well have added the reign of 'Bloody Mary', the Gunpowder Plot and some other incidents as further ingredients in the judgments passed by some of our fellow countrymen on the Catholic Church. Catholics in this country should know well enough what it is to have a 'bad image'. This should make them extremely careful about accepting the bad image of the Pentecostal Movement, whether as a phenomenon in their own Church or as part of a much wider phenomenon.

Certainly we cannot avoid having some prejudices. For a prejudice is but a judgment passed with inadequate knowledge of the phenomenon judged, and we are doing this all the time; and it is obviously impossible for us to become adequately informed on every new spiritual movement or philosophy that raises its head. Very often we have no serious call to do so. But when some such movement or philosophy invades our own spiritual patch, or even makes itself vigorously known in our neighbourhood, then we are compelled to react, and the hour for sorting out our prejudices

2

from our principles, and for distinguishing between genuine information and hearsay has arrived. It is all too easy to shut the door and decide that a movement that appears to be new, cannot concern us who enjoy possession of the truth from of old. From the days of Our Lord until now, it has been easier for spiritual have-nots to receive new enlightenment than for the haves, who hold doctrine with more rigidity than lovingness. Our Lord taught us to have always the docility – the teachableness of the child but how shall those whose business it is to teach retain such a quality? Yet Our Lord's instruction 'Unless you become like little children . . .' remains a permanent part of his message. The door has to be ever open, not indeed to any current of opinion but to what the Spirit may have to say to us, whether directly or through the words of others.

It is reasonable at this stage when innumerable persons in the Church claim to have received a total spiritual renewal (and among its adherents are cardinals and bishops), and when the Pope, the highest authority of the Church, has several times shown his benevolent interest, to invite unprejudiced persons and those whose prejudices are not unassailable, to consider what the Charismatic Movement has to say about itself.

It will be well to suggest certain canons of judgement. In the first place, one does not judge any religious movement primarily on the basis of anecdotes, stories or allegations about the behaviour of individual persons. On this basis all religious movements, – indeed all religions – would stand condemned. One starts by finding out what it has to say for itself, what it claims, what it offers. One considers also the overall picture of its life. Catholics have a right to feel annoyed if the picture of monastic life in their Church is made up of failed monks and nuns, without regard to the positive achievements of the monastic order or its genuine ideals. Indeed the enemies of the Church have always drawn heavily on such failures to prove that the whole idea was unsound. But in fact there is no religious area, and no Christian Church that has not spiritual failure to admit in its history. We claim however to be judged by what we teach, and by the effects that follow when our teaching is sincerely accepted. And this standard we should grant to the charismatic movement. Our judgement on this movement should not be based on bizarre stories (true or not), and odd personalities, but on an examination of its basic teaching, and the qualities of its best teachers, and the consequences of their teaching.

There is another preliminary point worth mentioning. It is sometimes suggested that charismatics are neurotic or troubled people brought together by a doctrine that promises comfort. And other general uncomplimentary characteristics are ascribed to them. However if we are examining sets of persons, we should be acquainted with the sociologists methods of judging them. This is best illustrated by an example. If, in a given group of 100 persons, twenty-five or more suffer from nervous diseases, that tells one nothing about the nature of the group, until comparison is made with another equivalent group (known to the sociologist as the 'control group'). Thus if in another similar collection of persons, the number of those suffering from nervous diseases is the same, more or less, the sociologists concludes that nervous disease is not a distinguishing feature of the first group. If the control group has a much lower figure of nervous sufferers, he would conclude that the first group was for some reason specifically subject to nervous disease; if the control had a higher figure then he would conclude that the group he was considering, was for some reason or other better placed than average. In fact when in a later book Fr Killian McDonnell applied this test to some charismatic groups in the USA, he found that they came out of it very successfully. Yet one would not want to deny that there is an attraction for the afflicted; Christianity is about that too.

Essentially the Charismatic Movement proclaims, not a new doctrine nor even a startling evolution of doctrine, but rather an event. It announces that the Holy Spirit is abroad

4

in our world today, offering a new and astonishing grace to all those who will accept it. It does not proclaim that the Holy Spirit was not at work before, for he is always at work in every age, having always a message for those who will hear him. But today the circumstances of the lives of believers have greatly changed in two ways. Although it is true that Christianity has been losing its position in the western world for three or four centuries, we observe a sharper battle, waged on more fronts, in our own times. Believers have their backs to the wall. Their enemies, that is the enemies of belief, are of every kind: they include doctrinaire militant atheists, governments of the right and of the left who make the profession of Christianity impossible, various kinds of profiteers from the trades of sin, civilised humanists. The discouragement arising from disagreement among Christians themselves is a further weakening factor. Moreover the huge advances in technology and science result in a general turning to science rather than religion as the answer to man's troubles; nor would any rational person want to reject the part that science has to play in the betterment of man.

Nor are the upholders of Christianity as sure of themselves as they were. What a quantity of books and articles appear almost daily, of which the aim is a reconsideration of traditional doctrines with a view to making them more acceptable to 'modern man'! This sometimes means a watering down of moral teachings, and a rationalisation of cherished beliefs.

No wonder that under these circumstances the faith of many is not equal to the strain put upon it, and that priests and ministers of religion so often feel unequal to the battle. Some give up as a result; more do not give up, but feel outnumbered, ill-armed and inadequate in the battle for the souls of men. The scales have tilted against them to an appalling degree; it is not strange if they feel depressed.

The other way in which the circumstances of believers have changed, and will change a great deal more, is that man

5

has a new awareness of himself. There is a good deal more to this than an awareness that he has achieved a technical-ogical mastery of his world, such that he can alter society and living conditions to an unheard of degree. For he has become aware that the human personality itself is capable of vast expansion, that it contains powers which now and again appear in some exceptional person (i.e. telepathy, second sight, telekinesis, etc) but are not understood as yet as a whole, and await development. We seem to be living in an age which in sober truth is a turning point in the history of man. Enormous possibilities of progress open up before us; so does the awful abyss of self-destruction.

In general: we have on our hands a sterner battle for the preservation of the Christian way of life. We sense also that it is an age of opening vistas for the future of mankind.

About all this the message of the Charismatic Movement is this:- Yes, the battle is on indeed, but do you not know, you who believe, that, corresponding to your needs, God has provided a new weapon for you? That there is a new and powerful grace offered to all who will accept it, one that reinforces faith, and gives new power against evil?

Pope Paul VI put the need we are faced with very clearly in certain significant questions: In our day [he asked], what has happened to that hidden energy of the Good News, which is able to have a powerful effect on man's conscience? To what extent and in what way is the evangelical force capable of really transforming the people of this century? What methods should be followed in order that the power of Gospel may have its full effect?

The Pope then had no doubt of the *hidden energy* of the Gospel; he refers to the need for *real transformation* as distinct from superficial profession, and he puts the question as to the *methods* (something we can select) by which the *power of the Gospel* (something God-given, always latently there) can be released to obtain the profound effects which faith calls for. And if these questions are not sufficiently clear, he puts the matter with almost desperate clarity: After the Council, and thanks to the Council, does the Church or does she not, find herself better equipped to proclaim the Gospel, and to put it into people's hearts with conviction, freedom and effectiveness?

While these questions were put by the Pope in the context of evangelisation, they are equally significant wherever the Church proclaims his message. Now no one could doubt that immense efforts have been made in search of new resources. A vast change has come over the liturgy, and therefore over the whole prayer-life of the Church. This is of extreme importance, but it is only one area: in canon law, in the life-style of the religious orders, in missionary activity, in theological teaching, and throughout her structures, we recognise earnest and sincere strivings towards that renewal of her vital energies, of her power to transform society through the Gospel, of which the Pope spoke.

The aim of renewal common to all these strivings is the adaptation of the Church to the needs of modern persons on the one hand, and the formation of better trained children of God on the other. These are like two sides of a coin. And it is obvious that in the end it is by the emergence of Christians of renewed vigour that the whole process will have to be judged. Debility in spiritual life would condemn, strength in spiritual life would justify the whole of these proceedings.

Hence we cannot afford to treat lightly or to dismiss as peripheral a movement which is concerned precisely with this objective, the renewal of spiritual life in itself. It spreads throughout the Christian world as a living impulse, unforced by any ecclesiastical authority, and seems in a way to be the renewal destined to give the breath of life to the other more official renewals. It claims to depend on the immediate action of God in human hearts; to be a stirring up of faith and of hope and of charity, and to give a new joy in the experience of the power of these supernatural gifts to overcome the world. It stands to be aided by structural, legal and ecclesiastical renewals, but also to bring new life to them. All spiritual life indeed depends on the Holy Spirit; he alone gives such life directly to human beings, and through them to programmes.

The spiritual renewal which makes its presence felt in the world today is not really a single thing but something more complex. The point which these pages will seek to make is that the movement known in this country as the Charismatic Renewal, and in France and Italy, simply as the Renewal, makes a contribution to this vast stream so valuable and significant that it cannot without grave loss be ignored. Its fundamental claim is that, through it (though not by any means only through it), the Holy Spirit is active today giving an abundance of new graces, corresponding to our numerous needs, and that through it we may draw near, accept and surrender, not to any human organization, for it is neither a Church nor an association within the Church, but to the Spirit of God himself. Those who ascribe to it do not think that the Spirit of God is conterminous in his action with their movement, or in some way peculiar to it. For the Holy Spirit acts where he wills; he does not confine his activity to any movement, and none can be more than an instrument of which he makes use. In fact charismatics feel themselves to be less a movement than a coalescence of persons who have felt themselves moved, that is affected, changed and even transformed, outside their own possibility of changing themselves, by the gratuitous action of God's Spirit. They do not as a body claim exclusive knowledge or exclusive rights in such a matter – to do so would be absurd and arrogant, but they do say: God has acted in us, we are witnesses to a new liberality in the showering of God's gifts upon those who will accept them. God acts very often in a corporate way, using those whom he has touched with his grace to help others. And therefore we wish to share this grace, this awareness of divine power, this infusion of divine joy, with our brothers and sisters in Christ. It cannot be otherwise since Christ's plan of salvation is essentially corporate: he adapts, aids and confirms us in grace through the actions of one another.

It is not then that they push a movement; at least that is not how they see it. Rather they are moved themselves. They cannot refuse to proclaim that God has been good to them personally and wills to be equally good to others. 'I wish before God that not only you but all who have heard me today would come to be as I am – except for these chains.' Thus Paul at his examination at Caesarea (Acts 26.29, Jerusalem Bible). Somewhat similarly the charismatic, whether he be capable of preaching the Gospel or not, whether he has made much progress or is still in an initial state of wonder, desires that the Goodness of the News should be experienced by all he meets. He is conscious of at least a beginning of the *transformation* in himself of which the Pope spoke, and knows what the Pope meant when he refers to the *hidden energy of the Good News*. The great new adventure of the Gospel in which he goes forward, like a child but holding the hand of God, has become intensely real to him.

The essential thing then of which we are talking is quite simply a grace, one which has the effect of bringing the whole Christian message into relief, as one would make the contrast between a map that is faithful but flat, and a model of the same country worked out in relief. The effect of the grace is then a deepening awareness of the reality of the Christian message and this deepening awareness is brought about by a stronger activity of the Spirit of Jesus within the person. This can be seen very clearly in the transformation of lapsed Christians not merely into churchgoers, but into persons conscious of a new joy in the practice of their faith. At the other end of the spectrum may be cited numerous cases of devout religious persons, whose life in Christ is renewed by a hitherto unexperienced warmth and consciousness of Christ's love for them personally. And there are plenty of us in between these categories who testify that the Lord has done new and unexpected things for us. These claims may provoke scepticism in others; and, for various reasons, some acceptable, some unworthy, do so. But can a serious Christian say that personal renewal is not necessary

9

for him? The alternative would seem to be to say (in suitable theological language no doubt): 'I am doing very nicely thank you.' In fact many do say this, even if for obscure reasons, they confess their sins from time to time; presumably they regard that as a minor matter like washing one's hands before dinner. But the realistic interpretation of Christianity is always to 'put off the old man', to be renewed, that is, made a 'new man', in Christ Jesus (Eph. 4.22, A.V.). That we are all called to this no one should doubt, nor that it is something we do not attain, but that must be simply accepted and joyfully received.

Where there is room for discussion is over the accepting of new arms in this warfare. No one can doubt that every grace received is a new event in the life of the receiver. But for some, it seems, that a grace, to be accepted, has to present itself in traditional form. If the Spirit has anything new to say to the Churches, which they doubt, let him be sure to make use of traditional methods. But can anyone so bind him? Who shall give directions to the Spirit of God? Let us start with a humble recognition of the Church's great needs today, and be ready to examine with humility the evidences that God is renewing its life through a new series of graces, great and wonderful, deep and transforming, in innumerable persons. Otherwise we might find ourselves appropriately addressed in the words of the Book of Job:

Who is this obscuring my designs
with his empty-headed words?
Brace yourself like a fighter;
now it is my turn to ask questions and yours to inform
me (Job 38.2–3 J. B.).

Happy are those Jobs who lose the battle with their God!

In essence the grace of renewal brings a new vitality to one's relationship with God and with the Lord Jesus. Like the pearl which St Ephrem describes in his famous poem it has various facets. St Ephrem thinks of himself as holding

10

in his hand the pearl of price of which the Gospel speaks (Matt. 13.45–6), and turning it over, and rejoicing in the diverse rays of light, the mysteries of the Kingdom, that it gives out. So somewhat the grace of which we speak has a number of different specific effects, it lights up with radiance themes that are common enough in spiritual literature. In particular it produces new repentance, joy, thanksgiving, surrender and commitment. All these experiences are deeply rooted in biblical teaching.

Repentance. Both Peter and Paul founded their apostolates on a deep sense of repentance – though neither had been what the world regards as 'a sinner'. Thus of Peter we read that 'the Lord turned and looked straight at Peter. . . . And he went outside and wept bitterly' (Luke 22.61). And Paul carried in his heart the consciousness: 'I am the least of the apostles, unfit to be called an apostle, because I persecuted the church of God' (I Cor. 15.9 Revised Standard Version).

The *thanksgiving* of Paul abounds in his letters, and not only for the graces given to his converts, but also for himself (Rom. 7.24) and such an expression as we read in 1 Peter 1.3, J.B.: 'Blessed be God the Father of our Lord Jesus Christ, who in his great mercy has given us a new birth as his sons, by raising Jesus Christ from the dead,' is an act of thanksgiving. Indeed all the blessings with which the letters of the New Testament proliferate should be recognized as acts of thanksgiving.

And then there is *joy.* As Peter says so significantly in his first letter: 'You did not see him, yet you love him; and still without seeing him, you are already filled with a joy so glorious that it cannot be described, because you believe, (I Peter 1.8, J.B.). St Paul was fully aware of the happiness he had brought his converts, and it was part of his teaching to show them how to preserve it. 'I want you to be happy, always happy in the Lord; I repeat, what I want is your happiness' (Phil. 4.4, J. B.).

The aspect of *surrender* may raise more problems for some persons. It will not do so for those whose previous lives

11

were not religious; for them the significance of surrender is clear enough. But for those already serving the Lord with devotion, what of them? Especially if they are already in the vows of religion? The answer is that we find that there are at any rate certain areas of our personality, or of our personal way of life, which in fact we have not surrendered, but reserved for our own good pleasure. Or we may find that the 'surrender' already made was far more superficial than we ourselves knew. It may be also that we *did* know, in an obscure and unwilling way, and could not cope, and so averted our attention, deceiving ourselves. Now comes the grace that enables us to complete what we wanted to do but could not. Not that this implies that we can complete it at once, but we are conscious of being on the move, as it is written: 'Rise up, take courage, the Master is calling you' (Mark 10.49).

The last facet we would mention is that of *commitment*, that is, we understand that this new grace is a call to a deeper life in Christ and to respond to it wholeheartedly. It is not necessary to quote either Peter or Paul to illustrate their demand that their converts should persevere in the grace that they had received. For those who already have persevered through years in the service of Christ, it is perhaps desirable to point out that for them this means acceptance of the new vistas that grace opens out before them. It does not imply rejection or even depreciation of all that has made up their past life; they will indeed see it somewhat differently, and the sense of thankfulness for all the graces received during it will deepen, but the new commitment is to the new incitements of grace, the new messages of love which the Lord sends through his own postal service. For some this may involve resolutions with external effects; for others the strengthened intercourse with their Master may be internal only; but not the less significant or real for that reason. This facet of new commitment is as essential to the grace of renewal as the repentance which we have listed first.

The above is the logical order of these perceptions. In

actual fact they do not always come in this order, for joy may come as a free gift first. Matthew sat down to feast with his Master first; if he did penance for his sins, as we must suppose, that came later. But the Son of Man dined with him, and a number of other sinners first, and he was not pleased with those who criticised his way of proceeding. The same thing can happen again; someone may receive the joy of feeling spiritually renewed, and yet the deeper conversion of which they are in need may take time to follow. It is certainly a law that it must take place and is an essential part of the divine will; but we cannot, must not, decide the order in which Christ distributes his graces.

Pervading these attitudes and indeed bringing them about is an *awareness of the love of the Saviour,* understood both ways. It is an awareness that he is loving us now, finding us in whatever corner of the earth we inhabit, and intent on drawing us to himself. It is an awareness too that he is conferring on us in some way a capacity to respond lovingly to this love. With the help of a little theology we realise that he is in some way conferring his Spirit upon us, that this Spirit is the lifegiver (the *vivificantem* of the Nicene Creed) who begins to produce livelier reactions in the soul than that person has ever experienced before. And they recognise, joyfully, that something is being done to them that they are totally incapable of doing for themselves: 'Thou shalt sprinkle me with hyssop, and I shall be cleansed; Thou shalt wash me, and I shall be made whiter than snow' (Ps. 50.9, Douai).

That sounds a quick progress and a purely passive one. In fact it may take longer, and it certainly calls for co-operation, yet the sinner is aware that something is being done to him, and not really by him. And he is aware of this divine love which is occupying itself with him, washing, purging, changing, not to be easily satisfied.

Is this process of an emotional kind? Sometimes indeed emotional experience comes quickly, but not always. The Saviour works in his own way on what he finds. Spiritual experience is definitely not to be identified with emotional

13

experience. Yet it is certain that the Saviour claims the whole of man, and that therefore he will at some stage call for and provide for an emotional response. To love without emotion is hard work anyway.

A final word about *joy*; the joy that is born of God. Unfortunately joy is often treated as if it were a merely emotional matter, and therefore some physical thing (rooted that is in the nervous system). Perhaps that is why our spiritual authors are given to teaching us to mistrust our spiritual joys and be content with our joyless aridities. This (whatever our authors may have intended) is a misleading half-truth. The joy that is born of God is to the soul as health is to the body. In point of fact the recovery of this joy is to many so extraordinary as to seem more or less miraculous. Yet it should not seem extraordinary that God should answer the prayer that the psalm puts on our lips:

Give joy to your servant, O Lord,
for to you I lift up my soul. (Ps. 85.4, Grail)

There are indeed cases, plenty of them, in which sadness and frustration have so taken possession of a person's soul that the entry of God's joy can only mean a change in personality so marked as to justify us in seeing there a wonderful exercise of God's healing power. But in itself God's Holy Spirit is a life-giving force and therefore essentially related to the joy of living. The psalms continually teach us that to live is to rejoice in God, because living is a sharing, at whatever distance, of God's life, and that his life is the source of all happiness. 'I never knew that you were meant to enjoy it,' said a lady after many years of faithful attendance at Church. Therein unconsciously she bore witness to what is lacking in so much religious practice. And joy cannot be manufactured from without; it is God's gift perceived within – something to be accepted from him.

A common but false notion is, that what those involved in the renewal movement call 'renewal in the spirit', is a

14

'summit' experience, or that there is a ceremony called 'baptism in the Spirit' through which aspirants receive a 'summit' spiritual experience. In fact the grace of renewal is the *beginning* of a new spiritual state characterised by a greater awareness of the nearness and reality of the divine promises. It is not necessarily conferred by the ceremony known as 'baptism in the Spirit'. It will be well to explain this further.

It is unwise to lay down any laws for the Holy Spirit, but we may reasonably seek for our own guidance to analyse the ways in which he acts. It seems then that in this grace, so frequent in our modern world, which we call spiritual renewal, he acts in one of three ways:

1. Without human intermediary. There is a personal encounter with the Lord, at once unforeseeable and unforgettable. Metropolitan Anthony in one of his books describes how as a young Marxist, he was provoked into reading a Gospel. He chose St Mark as it was the shortest, and during that reading he suddenly became aware that Christ was unmistakably present in the room with him. This experience altered his whole life.

A man employed as a ship steward told me how one day there came to him an almost compulsive grace. It invited him to give up certain practices, distinctly profitable and normal enough, but not easily reconcilable with his Christian conscience. He accepted the grace and the financial sacrifice involved, and another grace followed . . . and another. An intensive prayer life grew in him as he became more and more markedly the recipient of the gifts of the Spirit. Later he found his place in a charismatic group, but the working of renewal had begun sometime before; for him a ceremony of baptism in the Spirit could only mean his commitment to the graces already being given him.

Plenty of persons can be found to testify to the fact that a new period in their spiritual life began for them with a direct and unmistakeable intervention of divine grace. They are however a minority.

2. Sometimes the grace of interior renewal is received

through the ministry of a single person. That person prays with the other for their spiritual renewal, and this is experienced either at the time or afterwards. A man wrote to me: 'After those two prayer sessions seven months ago, the flood-gates of grace were opened to me. . . . What puzzles me still: Why does God give the way he does? I had done nothing, had in fact acted against him, yet he gave. I had not asked for love or forgiveness (such as I have received), yet both have been heaped upon me. I had not asked for his presence, yet he made it almost tangible, so near that I felt pain.' He had been a monk many years. The experience to which he referred was not instantaneous, but something that grew in strength as the days passed.

3. At charismatic meetings it is common for a group to pray over someone who desires to receive the grace of renewal. Sometimes indeed it is clear that the process has already begun, and in that case the object and significance of the prayer will be for its continuance and to enable the person prayed over to give their personal commitment to the Lord in response to what he is doing. But where renewal is not known to have begun and is being prayed for the procedure is described as praying for 'baptism in the Spirit'. It is not a sacrament; the persons who pray cannot actually confer it, as if it were a covenanted grace. All that they know is how to allow themselves to be channels of God's grace, so that through their agency the gift of renewal, a new awareness of God's inhabiting the soul and the consequences of this awareness, may be granted. Although this ceremony is often referred to as simply 'the baptism in the Spirit', not being a sacrament, it is not necessarily (or as the theologian says *ex opere operato*) effective. It happens that nothing happens; it happens that the person is conscious of profound sensations of the divine action; it happens that the person is conscious of nothing during the prayer, and yet afterwards becomes aware that from that time a new divine action began within him.

In general this is the commonest way in which persons

receive the grace of renewal, and through which they come to describe themselves as charismatics. Emotion experienced at the time may well be an accompaniment of the grace but is in no way a decisive proof; indeed this may depend partly on a person's temperament or that of those engaged in the prayer. If this is not what we should look for, what should we look for? Primarily we should look for the signs of divine power. And these are: (1) Those deep, interior, personal changes, which are in themselves invisible, but become manifest through words and actions and the various ways in which we recognize a changed personality. They may take time, of course, to declare themselves. (2) Those gifts of the Spirit which we refer to as *charismata*.

Any reader who has persevered so far may be justified in wondering whether the word *charismatic* is necessary at all. In fact it is only against the background of the foregoing explanations that the significance of the word can be appreciated. Otherwise we run the risk of either exaggerating or depreciating its importance.

For when, as we say, referring to the above process, 'the Spirit comes', he does not come without bringing spiritual gifts. The Greek name for these gifts is *charismata*. The *charismatic* is one who has received gifts of this kind.

Of what kind? We do not refer to sanctifying grace, which is received by all in baptism; nor are faith, hope and charity normally referred to by this name; nor yet again the traditional gifts of the Holy Spirit conferred in baptism. However when God has given us all that is necessary and essential for our salvation, he has still more to give. He can and does enrich the souls of those who ask him in uncountable ways.

Thus the gifts of the Spirit are of all kinds. Some are for the benefit of the individual, some for the building up of the Church at large. In fact what builds up the individual is also for the benefit of the community, and contrariwise a gift that is an aid to the building up of the community, should also be a fulfilment of the personality of the receiver. The two things cannot be entirely separated. Allowing however

17

for a certain distinction in their immediate aim, we may class among the first of these categories such things as a new love for and aptitude for understanding Holy Scripture; a new love for and aptitude for prayer; a new discernment of spiritual things; or, negatively, the disappearance of old temptations such as lust, bitterness, wordly ambitions, or involvement in worldy pleasures. Release, as by a touch of Christ, from deep psychological wounds is a common 'negative' gift. On the other hand there are gifts given mainly for the benefit of others, for the building up that is, of the Mystical Body of Christ. The brief list given in I Cor. 12. 4–11 is mainly of this kind. These so-called 'service gifts' do not confer new qualities, they strengthen a natural gift. For example an administrator may find that his natural talent for his task is mysteriously strengthened; a teacher may find his teaching capacity blossom in an unexpected way; the artist may find his insight more penetrating; the preacher may suddenly find that his gift receives a new dimension that does not escape his normal audience. The housewife too has her special needs whether as wife or mother; if Jesus had a special thought for her (Luke 15.8) the Holy Spirit has so no less; she may find that she copes more effectively and more joyfully with her problems and her anxieties.

Moreover there are certain gifts which are given because a person is called to be the carrier of a certain divine activity: such is the ministry of healing. A distinction is necessary here between the receiving of a special ministry of healing, which is relatively rare gift, and the learning how to co-operate in prayer for the needs of one another which should be a normal part of Christian life. If the reception of a full ministry of healing seems to be rare, answers to prayer for all sorts of needs, not excluding healing, become more common as faith grows. Particularly is this true of the prayer of a group.

It is well-known that *charismata* in the sense described include the gift of speaking in tongues, interpretations of this, prophecies, discernment of spirits and of maladies, and other unusual phenomena. This chapter, however, deals only with the question: What do we mean in general by 'this charismatic thing'? therefore the gifts will not be examined individually. It is more important to see the charismatic gifts as part of the larger picture. Otherwise we would get the impression that charismatics were persons *mainly preoccupied* with spiritual gifts. Now this would be wrong. It is particularly unfortunate if enquirers into the charismatic scene isolate such phenomena as speaking in tongues, singing in tongues, or prophecy, from their context. It is only by context that such phenomena are judged. The Bible gives us plenty of examples of strange and preternatural happenings of which God was not the author. 'There is a man working miracles in your name,' said the disciples to Christ, and he was content to say: 'Do not interfere with him.' But mostly such unauthorised persons are shown as coming to grief (Acts 19.13). Our Lord himself warned against false prophets and miracle workers who came in his name (Matt. 24.24); on the other hand he lists those signs that mark most clearly that his followers are treading in his footsteps. These are detailed in the parable of the sheep and the goats (Matt. 25.31–46). This is not the same as saying that the other signs are worthless – for Christ also indicated that they would be present among his followers: 'These are the signs that will be associated with believers: in my name they will cast out devils; they will have the gift of tongues; they will pick up snakes in their hands, and be unharmed should they drink deadly poison; they will lay their hands on the sick, who will recover' (Mark 16.17, J.B.). The point is that the fullness of Christianity calls for both. It always has done, and in theory, few if any Catholics would deny this. What we are concerned with today is that both types of sign should flourish together and abundantly. For then will the Church be enjoying that richness of life which her Master promised.

With this preliminary consideration then the value of the charismatic gifts becomes clear. They were present in the early Church in abundance; they have never deserted the

Church, though there have been great differences of degree and of kind in their manifestation. If now they are abundantly renewed, why should we hesitate to recognise them, and to thank him who alone can send them?

Pope Paul VI pondered this possibility aloud, when to a prepared text, he added the words:

> We cannot but hope that these gifts will come and with abundance; that in addition to grace there will also be charisms possessed and obtained by the Church today. The saints, especially the Fathers St Ambrose and St John Chrysostom have said that the charisms were more abundant in ancient times. The Lord gave his outpouring of gifts in order to give life to the Church, to make it grow, to establish it, to sustain it. And since then the granting of these gifts has been, I would say, more discreet . . . more economical. . . . How wonderful it would be if the Lord would again pour out the charisms in increased abundance, in order to make the Church fruitful, beautiful and marvelous, and to enable it to win the attention and astonishment of the profane and secularised world.[2]

Indeed a live, energetic, praying, loving and rejoicing Church is surely exactly what we need today. And if it is by the gift of his charisms that the Holy Spirit brings this about today – and there is plenty of evidence that this is so – why is that some people shy away from the very idea of a Christianity as rich today as it was in the beginning?

There are indeed quite a number of reasons for this, but before considering them let us sum up the ground covered. That the Church needs renewal in the sense of spiritual strengthening in the face of her battle, no one should deny – even if he has the most diverse ideas of how this strengthening is to be attained.

Concurrently with all the changes taking place to update

[2] General Audience, Oct. 16, 1974. Quoted from E. O'Connor *Pope Paul and the Spirit.*

20

the Church as a society, there is also this inmost need of the strengthening of the spiritual life in the heart of each person. Without this, little will be gained.

This too is apparent through God's grace in many places and persons throughout the world.

To this inner renewal the so-called Charismatic Movement makes an immense contribution; but it would be better to say that God works mightily through it, towards his end.

It is called charismatic because its followers expect and seek the *'pneumatika'* or *'charismatica'* set out in the New Testament as part of the life of the Church of God. They believe that these gifts of the Holy Spirit will be poured out on those who ask for them, and will contribute greatly to the richness of the Church.

If we accept the Holy Father as our supreme guide in spiritual matters, we should note that Pope Paul VI often sent messages of approval to charismatic gatherings, and if he uttered words of warning also, these were in the form of guidance and were not any sort of condemnation.

Two further general questions may be asked here.

1. Is the name Charismatic Renewal a good one? Or would 'Renewal' simply, or 'Renewal of the Spirit' be better? Both in France and Italy the word 'Renewal' alone is used.

There is something to be said either way. The disadvantage of the title *Charismatic Renewal* is that it puts a heavy emphasis on one aspect of the consequences of Renewal, whereas certainly it is 'Renewal in the Spirit' that is the key doctrine. On the other hand the word 'Charismatic' does underline something distinctive, namely that in this movement these specific gifts of the Holy Spirit are appreciated, even longed for and sought. Moreover the movement called Charismatic Renewal, by whatever name it goes, is not conterminous with spiritual renewal in the Church. The Spirit, as we have indicated above is not tied to any one set of persons, and does not so tie himself. By using the word 'charismatic' we designate a body of persons and the methods they use, and this clarifies what we are talking about. This

21

body of persons however is very loosely knit and it must not be assumed that there is only one method to be found in prayer meetings. Other names such as 'Pentecostal' have been proposed, but are also open to misunderstanding. This brings us to the other question:

2. Should these spiritual gifts (*pneumatika*) be sought? The answer in Scriptural terms seems to be a simple Yes: St Paul says 'Seek the spiritual gifts' (I Cor. 12.31) and the word so translated is a strong one (*Zeloute*), which can hardly be translated 'We should have an appreciation of these spiritual gifts (but stop very short of seeking them)'. Do not a whole legion of spiritual writers occupy themselves in warning us not to be presumptuous and expect God to do anything special for us? They do indeed, but must not be allowed to stand between us and Scripture. Our Lord says that, much more than an earthly father, will our Father who is in heaven give good things to those who ask him! (Matt. 7.11). Presumably this refers to all the range of the blessings of the Holy Spirit. St Peter too urges us along the same path: 'Long for the pure spiritual milk that by it you may grow up to salvation; for you have tasted the kindness of God' (I Peter 2.2 R.S.V.).

Fr Faber in an interesting chapter in his *Growth in Holiness* (1854) observes a difference between ancient and modern authors with respect to the seeking of divine favours and consolations. The latter he says are for ever cautioning us against wanting, let alone praying for such things, whereas the earlier authors exhort us to seek and pray for them.

After a lengthy discourse, he comes down cautiously on the side of the ancients. From our standpoint of today one feels that these authors are all to be judged by their context, by the audiences for whom they wrote and the prevailing spiritual climate in which they wrote. But it is interesting that Fr Faber should have felt the need for such a discussion and, although he wrote at a time which we are apt to pass over as less spiritually open then our own age, the question he asks is remarkably relevant here. There is certainly a division of attitude in such matters. Many devout persons have a feeling that any seeking of specific spiritual gifts of their own choosing conflicts at a level deeper than discussion with that total submission, surrender and *abandon* of their whole person to God, which is the basis of their entire spirituality. This sentiment is not to be treated disrespect-fully. But it is also true that the desire for spiritual gifts is not necessarily and should not be just the product of our desire for personal fulfilment. It may be a desire placed in our hearts by the Spirit of God so that he may act in us more powerfully for the building up of the Body of Christ. We have then to accept such desires, to purify them of self-interest, and to realise that we are put on earth to be the instruments through whom God carries forward his plans. And to be such instruments we need to be enriched by his gifts. Otherwise we are like soldiers whom no one has armed. Yet the reasons why spiritual authors came to warn more than to encourage about these things were very serious ones:

1. The dangers of illusion – of developing a false mys-ticism. No doubt this was the motive that caused the half dozen directors of St Teresa's conscience to advise her to insult her visions of Christ.

2. The danger of stopping still on one's way to God because of spiritual favours received on the way. This might be summed up: do not admit any spiritual consolations lest they distract you from the direct intent on God alone.

3. The fact that those who believe themselves to receive instructions or communications direct from God, tend to see them as to be obeyed and accepted whatever the attitude of their human superiors.

However it is possible too that we have been over-warned. Too much caution against laying oneself open to divine favours will lead us to espouse aridity; aridity in its turn begets weariness, and weariness weakness. There are plenty of dangers along this path too. For example – the notion that the approach to God must be a disagreeable business, mainly a matter of penance, austerity and all that human nature finds hard; a notion that any enjoyment of the Good News is to be avoided; an unconscious assumption that God must be parsimonious in his good things which all have to be earned the hard way; and not least, an ignorance of the powers that Christ wills to exercise in his kingdom through its members. Surely this kind of thinking makes Love's way harder than Christ made it? Granted that it is in a real sense a narrow way, is there not a danger of making it narrower still, so that even fewer find it?

Perhaps one might sum this up by saying that a stylised form of sanctity has replaced the broader simplicity of the New Testament. Dangers have been scientifically eliminated, and the science of holiness so formed remains narrow and impoverished, lacking the fullness of the New Testament 'parresia', boldness, confidence.

One sign of this 'divide' is that Catholics often derived their spiritual instruction from secondary sources, rather than from the constant reading of the Scriptures. If they read them they did not receive joy from their message; it seemed too remote from their actual situation.

There is a 'divide' too in the attitude to healings, which may be explained thus: One way of conceiving God is to think of him as the supreme Spirit who having made the universe and invested it with its laws, cannot reasonably be expected to intervene personally, except on the rarest occasions. He may do it occasionally for an exceptionally holy person, or even show his power at the rare shrine. But it is not proper for ordinary folk to be constantly expecting him to intervene on their behalf. The charismatic approach on the other hand works on the implications of God having sent his Son and committed 'all power and authority on earth' into his hands. That means that Jesus is in control of every situation; it all concerns him; we do not understand exactly how, but we are sure of this, and sure therefore that we may rely on his promise to be our shepherd in all circumstances. The only law that counts is *his* will. The one thing necessary

24

then is to learn how to do his will in our actual circumstances, expecting in return the fullness of his promises
whether this corresponds to what we call normal or not.
Normality is to be identified with his will. There is of course
a mystery here since as we know his full taking possession
of his universe is not complete. But that precisely is achieved
through the growth of faith in him. For many healing is an
aspect of redemption; it is therefore part of his normal will;
but this his will is brought into actuality by the exercise of
our faith. To grow in him is to seek healing through him.
There is for many a certain newness in this attitude which
finds it natural that Christians should pray for *and expect*
healing.

There is however nothing in this which suggests a rejection of the Christ's doctrine that we are invited to take up
our cross and follow him (Matt. 16.24). Suffering in itself is
part of the kingdom of darkness, as illness is the little brother
of death. Christ our master suffered that he might overcome
suffering; thus he freed us from the kingdom of darkness
and its consequences. Hence there is a suffering which we
are called on to share with him in his redemptive task, and
there is a suffering which is the fruit of the kingdom of
darkness, and keeps back the coming of Christ's kingdom.
Against suffering recognised as the work of the kingdom of
darkness still at work in this world we react then by asking
to be delivered from it ourselves so that we become capable
of attacking its spread among others. We look for our own
healing through the triumphant power of Christ, so that by
the elimination of our wounds we may face up better to trial
in the battle for Christ which is the lot of the Christian. It
is one thing to bear the cross, another thing to be such
cripples that we cannot bear it. It is one thing to accept
redemptive suffering in ourselves, another to feel totally
helpless in the presence of the sufferings of others.

Another point in which the advent of interior renewal
marks a new attitude in the Christian is that it develops his
sense of responsibility. If it does not do this, it is at best a

superficial experience, and does not really deserve the name of renewal. For the grace itself implies a recognition of one's Christian responsibilities. They are not new responsibilities; what is new is that they are perceived clearly, and accepted.

The first of these is to the Gospel. It demands to be spread. It admits of no neutrality. There should not be three classes: those who accept and spread the Gospel, those who are ignorant of it or reject it, and those who accept it but are passengers in the Kingdom of Christ. The Gospel has this latent power, that as it is absorbed, so it is perceived to be vitalising, that is, life-bringing to the person who has absorbed it; it cries out within him: 'I am for others too.' The old philosophers had an adage: Good is naturally diffusive of itself. Much more so is this true of Christ's Good News. Inevitably when it has become a vital joy-bringing experience in a human heart, it arouses that person to bring his discovery to another.

This means then that there must grow a sense of responsibility to one's neighbour. It is not always there at first. A person involved in renewal may be filled with joy, and gifted with tongues, and yet not grasp fully the responsibilities of a Christian. That will seem to critical eyes an unsatisfactory position, but the Spirit of God does not always act in the order which we would prescribe for him; sometimes he begins with a large dose of encouragement, so that the person may be helped by this in the more essential task of growing in Christian responsibility. First he says: 'Drink this', then he says: 'Now begin to walk.'

In general a sense of responsibility will bring a person beyond the idea of just receiving something good for themselves to the acceptance of the duty of bringing all the good in his power to fellow-Christians. And this in its turn will imply growth in a new learning. Part of this learning concerns the Christian life he leads himself, part concerns the art of helping other persons. This will mean growing both in the courage to carry the cross and simultaneously in the joy of sharing the triumph of the Resurrection.

2 The Priest and the Charismatic Movement

Many priests are ill-informed about the charismatic movement. 'All we know about this sect is that opinion everywhere condemns it' said the Roman Jews to Paul (Acts 28.22, J.B.). Evidently they had heard of some new and divisive teaching, but were in no hurry to get involved. There are reactions like this today, when there is talk of renewal. But it is well known also that in a world in which religious bodies generally admit their losses in numbers and influence, the phenomenon called Pentecostalism alone increases in both respects. It exists inside what are described as main-line churches and makes progress, even up-stream. In the Catholic Church it must surely be recognised as the most challenging event of the day, and not least challenging in this that it advances unchallenged – but not unobserved or unconsidered – by the highest authorities. It has in fact met with much less opposition in the Catholic Church than in some other Christian bodies. This is partly because the Catholic Church has in the course of her history been the home of the most numerous forms of spiritual experience; and partly because there is in her theological teaching no resistance to the idea of the intervention of the supernatural. This attitude which makes acceptance of supernatural phenomena theoretically easy is balanced by a kind of practical scepticism in concrete cases, as the trials of the youthful Bernadette of Lourdes illustrate.

In general the attitude of the Catholic episcopal hierarchies to the Charismatic Movement has been sympathetic; often it has been encouraging, sometimes it has given paternal guidance, sometimes it has kept silence, but never, I think, has it issued a condemnation.

Since parish priests soon become aware of the trials, or the problems or the joys of their flock, sooner or later any parish priest will find himself having to react to 'this charismatic thing'. Inevitably his judgment, like all such judgments, will reflect his temperament and training. He may decide quite simply to find out first hand what it is all about. Or his judgment may be kindly but negative: 'It may help some people, so I suppose it's all right for them. But I have as much work on my hands as I can personally carry.' Or it may be less kindly: 'From what I have heard, it is all very dubious, even pernicious. I never touch anything of that sort'; or it may resemble that of the French Bishop in whose diocese Dom Guéranger founded in 1833 the first monastery after the French Revolution: 'Madame' he wrote to a friend, 'a monastic epidemic has broken out in my diocese.'

The parish priest who finds that a charismatic epidemic is breaking out in his parish or threatening to do so, has then a problem on his hands. He may be happy about it or the reverse; as a shepherd he can hardly be indifferent; he may be suspicious (that is in fact quite a normal starting point), but he will not deny his parishioners the right to meet together to pray. He may think it odd that a sudden desire to meet for prayer invades some of his parishioners, but it is hardly an adequate response to be content to distrust 'all that sort of thing'. He may indeed have reasons for doubts; the existence of such a prayer group is *prima facie* proof of only one thing – it is evidence of some kind of thirst for spiritual things, even for an experience of divine things. It marks too a feeling that attendance at even the most sacred of our services has not brought them the answer they seek: some element – call it for want of a better word – tuition or instruction at the level of the heart – has not been found. Now such desire is surely legitimate desire: seen on the large scale it is a massive desire of humanity for God; seen on the

28

small scale it is something that calls for the priest's care. It is his business to examine with sympathy, if he is not already well informed in the matter, the significance of these spiritual thrustings. It is not necessarily one more job for him to be saddled with, or something for him to take over, but it is some thing of deep significance. It may be the best thing that has happened spiritually for many a day; it may be a false track; or again it may be good in itself, but something that will need guidance. These are concrete questions with differing answers in different places.

Let us place ourselves in the position of a parish priest who is confronted with this problem. He may well have heard and read that this charismatic business is dangerous (with some authenticated stories to prove the point) and therefore something to save his parishioners from. He may well have heard that it changes people profoundly, turning harsh persons into gentle ones, arrogant persons into humble ones, making loving persons out of loveless ones, and even ardent churchgoers out of lapsed Catholics; that it is not in fact just a devout association, nor a pietistic society or new prayer method. He may well have met some person or persons claiming to be 'charismatic' and is likely to be affected quite strongly in his judgment by his impression, favourable or unfavourable, of their behaviour and person- alities – and, by and large, parish priests are shrewd judges of spiritual attainments. Moreover he is bound to know that a large number of his fellow clergy – in this country certainly some hundreds – are involved.

This last fact alone will strike him as significant. For it means very obviously that the appeal of the movement can- not be explained as a matter of a certain type of temperament, or of ignorance of theology or of sensation-mongering. For, by and large, priests (especially parish priests) are a practical lot, knowing very well the difference between genuine good- ness and mere spiritual exaltation. Nor are they short of things to do. Theirs is a life of many facets – the pastoral care of souls, the celebration of Church services, preaching, the upkeep of Church property, the financial struggle, the multifarious forms of special apostolate in school, hospital, prison, or even lunatic asylum, and much more – and withal, the need (as we say) to keep up one's spiritual life. Above all there is the sense of responsibility for the well-being of their flock; and how hard and heavy á burden that can be!

If then there are priests in growing numbers who testify to the personal benefit that has come to them and to the transformation that has come over their work through their being involved in the charismatic movement, their witness is not to be treated lightly. For these men are in the firing line, and know very well what the battle is about. Books are useful in their way, but without question no one is better qualified to explain the nature of the grace of renewal to a priest than a priest who has himself received this grace. For he has been through much the same growth processes as any other priest, has used the same theology books up to his ordination, and done the pastoral work that follows ordination: he knows all about the deceptions, the frustrations and the rejections that are involved in his work. He among all others has found out for himself that human good will and talent and training are not of themselves adequate to win the battle with human sin and sloth and the whole conspiracy of evil that he is up against; he knows, none so clearly, that divine power is the only answer. He has indeed by virtue of his ordination a certain equipment and a conferred power to do essential things. He is conscious too of his own talents and of his faith, and almost certainly from time to time he knows moments of consolation and of victory. But is it enough? If God's ordnance department has produced a new weapon apt for his form of front-line warfare, should he not examine it hopefully? After all, is not that exactly what the situation calls for? Much work goes on for re-structuring this and producing a new look for that, but what he needs most of all is an empowering grace enabling him personally to work more effectively for the salvation of those quite ordinary people among whom he spends his life. He knows absolutely that his task is too great, his burden too heavy, that the tide of infidelity sweeps strongly against his flock; may be he consoles himself with the thought that he does as well or no worse than others, the Bishop cannot expect any more. . . . But if a loving God is bringing to him new possibilities of touching hearts, of saving souls, what then? It is worth surely an investigation, and more than a cursory one. Too much is at stake.

The first issue in his mind will surely be the question: Is this based on sound theology? If that hurdle is passed, there will still be questions concerning its practical value. In fact the last chapter dealt with theological matters. This one will consider mainly the practical issues. So let us consider three things: What the priest stands to gain personally; what he may hope to gain in his professional work, and finally, objections that may reasonably cause him to hesitate.

On the personal level the priest is but a man like any other, and therefore his spiritual problems may be as diverse as other mens. But there are two or three connected with his profession about which a few words may be useful.

In recent years we have seen many priests give up the priesthood, and the reasons have been very diverse. Many of them have by no means given up the faith; rather they have withdrawn from the front line, from the arduous task of caring for others. So many questions about so many aspects of life calling for answers! The burden of being expected to provide reassurance to every one else, when one is bothered by the same questions, even the same doubts! The burden of consoling the suffering without the power to do so! Is one a hypocrite if one perseveres in such tasks and feels an unconfessed inadequacy in the course of them? It is only natural if not a few withdraw from such responsibilities. They test the depth of personal faith and of charity too; under modern conditions the priest's ministry will be a heavy burden indeed unless he is capable of sustaining others. And the pressures on his faith and charity are intense. There is no reason to suppose that they will lessen.

31

What an immense advantage to a priest then, if he receives a profound strengthening of his faith through a new awareness of the nearness of Christ, of the power of Christ working through him! Many priests know something of this already without reference to our special theme. But why stop there? They can safely encourage themselves with the knowledge that there is more, always more, and that this more is available and will be given. They, if any one, need to experience the truth of Our Lord's promise that if we ask our Father he will have good gifts for us (Matt. 7.7). But something may be needed to start off this new activation of their faith and new confidence in prayer. Priests who have found what they needed through the charismatic movement will say to them: 'We have found it by this means.' As we are members of the Mystical Body, we should be able to help one another forward by the sharing of our problems, and also of the answers. But the best answer is the sharing of Christ himself through the communication of his grace in prayer. For argument and discussion are but a prelude, counsel may help somewhat, but it is in prayer together that the real strides forward are made. This kind of help many priests can give to their brethren.

Let us turn to another difficult area in a priest's life. One reason why he has to work so hard today is that he works in a world organized to a large extent to render chastity as difficult as possible. (And let it be noted that whatever is opposed to chastity will also undermine faith.) He not only works in this world: he lives in it. It is all around him, presenting its maxims and its enticements to his senses in a way that must be unprecedented since the pagan world finally surrendered to Christianity. Hoardings in the street, magazines and periodicals in the shops and kiosks, cinemas, theatres, television in the house . . . need one name all the media by which the message of sexuality is proclaimed? This is sometimes presented as a readjustment after years of over-repression of the natural instincts of man, a new and beautiful liberty. In fact the whole campaign of pressures rises from

32

something much more mercenary than that. But the point here is just this: this is the world with which the priest has to struggle, and in which he has to live. And he is a celibate. And in all probability he is going to be lonely. Loneliness added to frustration is a tough combination: add all the incitements to seek earthly compensations – be it in drink or sex or whatever – and it is no exaggeration to say that a priest – who is but a man – really needs the divine protection and the divine encouragement. We all need these things, but in his case the need is seen to be great and urgent. Again we may say: plenty of priests no doubt rejoice in having received what they need in this way – but not all. In any case there is more to be had for the seeking. It is one of the effects of spiritual renewal that it deals powerfully with the internal situation. Indeed where there is tension and weakness, the relief of this is likely to be its first effect. For God's workman needs to be relieved, comforted and refreshed in himself, before he can bring these things to others. And it is through receiving such graces that he learns how in faith to bring them to others. He has a claim on God to give him the strength of soul that his position requires. But this means that he must taste God's power working in him, healing him of his own weaknesses, and enabling him to say with the psalmist:

God is my rock: in him I am secure.

God is my joy; in him I find happiness.

This is truly part of his equipment whether for fighting evil things or lifting up the fallen. There is really nothing new in this; what is new is, on the one hand a new virulence in the adversaries, and a new and answering largesse of his grace and his power on God's part to those who accept that they need it, and are willing to go in search of it. Such a largesse, or, to refer back to a metaphor already used, such a new weapon is something that God owes his modern priest. It is not confined to the charismatic renewal; God is not confined to any set of persons. But we do say that God does grant such graces through this movement, and that the priest who seeks may well find renewal there. For God works through human beings, passing grace through us to one another; that is what the doctrine of the Mystical Body of Christ is about. We come to find what it really means by stepping forward to share our needs and our graces with one another.

A lot of us have difficulty in praying. And some of us are secretly envious of others who apparently have a real appetite for it. In this respect there is no difference between a priest's problem and anybody else's. But he is different to this extent that *his* need for prayer is an imperative; he is usually aware of this, and more or less unhappy if his prayer life has come to a stop, like a clock that needs winding, if one could but find the key. This key is to be renewed spiritually. In the charismatic renewal movement the priest may well find his key. It is, so to speak, a good place to look for it.

Then there is loneliness, with its effects on the personality. For the priest is in a dilemma. Like everybody else, he needs love, both to give it and receive it. If he does not give and receive love, he is liable to shrivel up into a lifeless functionary. Clearly as a celibate he is restricted in this matter. But the whole problem is much deeper than that. The real problem is how can he love God's people, giving himself in love to individuals (men and women) as well as to his whole flock. He has to find in himself a love that is real, self-giving, joyful – and yet not possessive. For they are God's lovely people not his own, and not for his possession. Now only Christ can teach him this; others may teach him about it. But only Christ can plant in him and water in him and make to grow this love which is really an authentic extension of the love of Christ himself. Christ did not use people to staunch the wound of his loneliness; neither should his priest; that would be to abuse Christ's people to satisfy a personal need. He has then to learn the reality of Christ's love for human beings by sharing it, and to know that he is rich by also sharing Christ's too, and – marvellous privilege – accepting likewise in some way the love of these people himself, being to them in the person of Christ.

And that is not loneliness. Moreover it puts the debate on celibacy into a different context.

This grace too implies a special gift of Christ; some priests indeed will already enjoy it. Others will need to seek it in spiritual renewal.

The release of the Spirit in him will bring the priest not only new strength in trial and temptation, but will help him with the professional aspects of his life.

To begin with prayer is not only an essential part of his own life as a priest, but he has a duty to pray for his people. He is an intercessor on their behalf. An understanding of this duty, a growing sense of responsibility about it, accompanied by a growing confidence in the fruit of his prayer, all these things are to be accomplished in him. It will take time for him to reach his full stature, to realise himself that Jesus awaits his prayers for his people and is a very good listener. It is easy to use words that may sound to a thoughtful reader an over simplification of this mystery of the prayer that prevails with God. All that I want to indicate here is that among the fruits of the release of the spirit for the priest will be the growth of his role of intercessor for his people. It may at the beginning seem a burdensome role, but as he perseveres, it will be his joy. In this too he shares in a sacerdotal way, the role of Christ the intercessor, not only in calling on Him, but also sharing with Him. Of this he will be increasingly conscious in his special role as celebrant of the Eucharist. And as it is a sacrament of intercession, so it is a sacrament of healing.

There is so much that the priest stands to gain from the release of the Spirit in his ministry. Carrying with him a new sense of the victory of Christ within himself, and an awareness of the presence of Christ his master, he has a new confidence, but not based on his own personal gifts; and he finds his priestly powers increased in ways that astonish him. It is not that there is any difference in those graces covenanted in the Sacraments; absolutions are not more complete, marriages are not more valid, nor baptisms more comprehensive. The grace that lies in the Sacrament as a covenanted sign is always there. But in addition to this, there is an uncovenanted side to every priest's work, also when he is working through the sacraments. So we are all aware that God works effects through some priests more than through others, or works diversely in different priests. It is in this ministerial area that the priest will find mysterious changes taking place.

Let us list some of these possibilities. They can only be put forward in a general way since what the Holy Spirit does in each priest varies as the Spirit himself wills. Nor will any mention be made here of gifts or *charismata* which the priest may share with the laity. It is with the ministerial side of the priest's life that we are immediately concerned.

Preaching: The priest will find that the Spirit of God informs his preaching in a mysterious way, opening up to him and thence through him the significance of the Scriptures. This however is not likely to take place unless he also finds time for some reading and study of the Scriptures for his own instruction. To speak with total conviction that this is Christ's message may or may not be new to him; after all our personal histories vary. But following the release of the Spirit many priests become aware of a difference, at least of degree, in the conviction with which they can deliver Christ's message; and some have a particularly strong feeling that even as they speak, it is given to them to speak what they are to speak. This is not prophecy, for it is still their own gifts that they are using, and their own sermons that they are preparing. But it is as if their gifts were touched now by a certain radiance of the Holy Spirit. When this happens it is not long before the congregation becomes aware of it!

The Sacrament of Reconciliation: In carrying out this sacrament the priest may acquire (perhaps a better word would be 'receive'), and should seek to develop a new capacity – to heal as well as to absolve his penitents. It is not that one absolution can be more complete or powerful than another; there can be no difference there, for the priest mediates forgiveness on behalf of Christ. But priests know all too well that often they are not able to reach the root of sin, that is, the wounded condition of the penitent's mind or psyche, that seems to make the sin more or less inevitable. This applies to such conditions as bitterness, despair, lust (whether normal or perverted) and in fact to a whole list of moral sicknesses. The penitent indeed is forgiven, but the sinner is not healed. The craving or irritation or trauma remains as powerful as before. The penitent returns to his tensions, from which there seems no way out except by falling again. Now the grace of renewal opens a door in the priest's mind, showing him that he like his Master is called on also to heal. When Christ said to the penitent woman who had anointed his feet: 'Go in peace; your faith has made you whole' (Mark 5.43, Douai), he used the same formula as he frequently used for a physical healing; but there was no physical healing in this case – only a moral one. He meant that through her faith and the application of his power she left his presence healed of the wound of lust. It is this power latent in the ministry of the priest which he has to learn to cultivate. The first thing is to grasp what is wanted. In fact priests know very well what their penitents want; so that one may say that the first thing to be grasped is that it is within their ministry to relieve these needs. To say that it is within their ministry is not to say that they can do this automatically relying exclusively on their ordination powers. It is a gift of Christ; something to be sought of him who promised to relieve and refresh the burdened who came to him (Matt. 11.28–9), something that will surely grow as a priestly power, as the confessor himself increases in Christlike love of humanity, and confidence in the knowledge that his Master works his works of spiritual healing through him. If only he, himself, understands the gift of God! Is it not *to him* that people come that through him they may be relieved of their heavy loads, to him precisely because in the sacraments lie the powers of Christ?

The Sacrament of Anointing the Sick: Properly speaking nothing can be added to the powers contained in the Sacrament. It is all there already. Yet, as with the Sacrament of the Eucharist, there are great and perceptible differences in the power which Christ manifests through it on different occasions or for different persons. It was said of him that when he came to Nazareth, he could work few miracles there because of their lack of faith (Mark 6.5), and there must be a lot of such Nazareths among our churches today. There is then a correlation between the liveliness of faith and the manifestation of divine power. This may seem almost a truism, but, through the gift of renewal in the Spirit, the faith of the priest becomes more living; his new sense of the nearness of Christ enlarges his compassion; he approaches the Sacrament of Anointing more expectantly and more confidently than before; he communicates his own confidence and faith to the sick person. One way or another (for we know that the sick are not *always* to be restored to physical health) priest and sick person alike find that their confidence is not misplaced. And physically too, through their greater faith, the power of Christ is more likely to be released; that is the implication of St Mark's text. But the priest's faith is not something stimulated for the occasion; it is something he brings with him, a permanent possession for all occasions, and a possession that is entirely submissive in all its expectancy to whatever may be the will of Christ on each occasion.

Truly the priesthood is a many splendour'd thing.

The Charismatic Movement may be of great assistance to the parish priest in that it offers him, a renewed man himself, a means of spreading renewal among his parishioners. It is by no means unknown for them to have preceded him. Indeed the movement seems to be the means by which today, among ordinary people torpor is changed into ardour, and boredom into joy; and, where is already religious interest and fervour, devout persons become empowered by new gifts to draw others into the same stream of renewed spiritual life. If then the priest has new confidence and joy in his heart, this will not mark a widening separation of experience between him and his flock. For through the charismatic prayer group the same largesse of divine grace brings new joy and the love of divine things to the hearts of his parishioners. They indeed wonder more and more at the (to them) novel way in which the Lord works in their hearts, drawing them closer to him, and therefore closer to one another, and inspiring them to go out and perform all manner of service in his name. The parish priest finds himself the centre of a growing number of people who are now ardent Christians, filled with that love which was so ardent a sign of the early Church, persons markedly drawn to the Eucharist and showing forth in their daily lives the fact of the Mystical Body of Christ. He will of course have his part to play in guiding them along these paths, but as it is necessary that he should be equipped to guide, so it is necessary that they be equipped to follow. They are likely to have lay leaders too. The reason is this: a group of lay-persons being a sample of humanity will contain persons gifted naturally in all sorts of ways. It follows that some have a capacity for leadership. The Holy Spirit who claims for his service the *whole* personality of man, touches with his fire these gifts also, and they feel urged to make use of them in God's service. The priest is accustomed, as a rule, to the problem of poverty; that is to say he works with a laity all too busy using their gifts in a hundred and one ways, to have much time to help him, and who also do not feel gifted to do so. He will then have to adapt himself to the problem of divine wealth pouring itself into the human vessels around him.

And on the level of human relationships, if the priest has had a problem of loneliness it will disappear, as he finds himself united in a conspiracy of joy with his parishioners, and finds himself surrounded by a new love diffused among

39

many hearts, yet substantially the same love. And he will feel himself also drawn to them with new love as he recognises the lively working of Christ in them.

Is this drawing too idealistic a picture? Of course it is. But it is dealing with new realities all the same. This is illustrated by St Paul's letters to the Churches he founded. They are realist and deal with the sins, the short-comings, even the illusions of the early Christians, but they give us a picture of a Christianity very spiritually alive, if also very human. Indeed as long as Christ's Kingdom is in its present stage it will always be the scene of combat between light and darkness; between grace and sin. And so we must expect that this combat with all that it implies of struggle with human egoism, human bitterness, human sensuality, delusion etc., will go on; indeed it will wax more lively. Christianity does not cease to be fire upon earth, and human society will always be a battlefield. The victory of Christ is not just a victory *over* us, nor merely a victory *for* us; it is also *through* us. And when Christ battles in us, whether individually or collectively, the going is not necessarily smooth and downhill. It is of the very essence of Christ's triumph that out of such poor human material as we are, he eventually evolves his victory; and sometimes it is not 'eventually', for he does it now, sweetly, compellingly, triumphantly, that we may know that he is Lord.

We share then in the *working* of Christ's triumph, not only in the enjoyment of the fruits of it. A parish in which Christ works a great work of renewal, will then be a live parish, one full of joy and compassion, and healing, and brotherly love. But it would be unrealistic to suppose that such results are handed down from heaven ready made. The way forward is marked also by struggle, sometimes by falls, and usually by some errors and setbacks, as well as by successes. It is sign-posted by gifts and graces, but we may at times find difficulty in reading the sign-posts. 'In all these things,' says the Apostle, 'we overcome on account of him who loved us.' We should expect to know both grief and joy – these

40

being the concomitants of being alive. Christ himself knew both. What is promised is to enter into his life even now here on earth; what is not promised is to enjoy eternal rest this side of eternity, nor that pale illusion of total peace which haunts us like a will-of-the-wisp, but is in effect reserved for the day when we share in Christ's own triumph.

*****

Parish priests – and other priests – may well have reservations about the charismatic movement, reservations based on their theological formation. The first such objection might be worded thus: Is not the charismatic following an 'illuminist' tradition of dubious orthodoxy? A tradition that makes an excessive appeal to the individual's personal experience of God, and suggests that to have such experience is to be superior to authority, and even in a superior position vis-a-vis of dogmatic belief? To say this is to put the question – deliberately – in a loaded form. Certainly those for whom their own individual experience of God is their exclusive rule of belief, cannot be recommended as guides for others. We have to part company with those who do not believe that God's plan of salvation is corporate, and therefore involves submission to those constituted in authority.

The issue however may be expressed more fairly by dividing it into two questions:

Is experience of God important in religion?

Do charismatics exaggerate its importance? Or the importance of their own experiences?

The answer to the first of these questions seems to be this: All the Bible is about experience of God. From the patriarchs onwards we are shown how God teaches men through the experience of himself. The Bible is not like Greek philosophy, an intellectual hunt for the truth, nor even a reasoned exposition of it. Jacob wrestles with God, who leaves his mark upon him (Gen. 32.26). Our Lord himself is not a philosophy, but a person to be known. And he is 'the image of the Father' whom we learn to know through him. It follows that we cannot have too much experience of God. We need all he will grant us, and as a general principle, he gives in proportion to our seeking. All the saints are persons who sought God with singlemindedness, and bear witness to their experience of him. The oldest religious orders owe their existence entirely to the desire to know God better in order to serve him better. In the long run these two things are inseparable. For if we serve God zealously this leads to a greater knowledge of him, supposing always that such knowledge is the real end of our zeal. He gives this knowledge or experience of himself diversely to diverse kinds of people: to the Bishop, or to the theologian, or to the monk; to the peasant woman or to the child. Religion without experience of God is a dessicated thing; it will become a lifeless thing, degenerate even into a business, as Kierkegaard insisted to the horror of contemporary Danes. Perhaps reflection will show us that we are also in danger of this. Properly understood then there can be no question of the importance or the rightness of seeking the experience of God. So indeed we are instructed to pray: 'It is your face O Lord that I seek' (Ps. 26.8, Grail)

It is sufficient to examine the prayers of the liturgy to see that they have been composed to lead us to pray for divine experience as something that is definitely expected. Divine consolation is expected too: a well-known collect ends with the petition 'that we may always be filled with the consolation of the Holy Spirit'. The first truth then to be established is that divine experience is to be desired, and therefore to be sought. Christ became man that in him we might experience the goodness of God. Indeed such experience is necessary for us if we are to do more than drag along with blistered feet in the way of the divine commandments. For this teaching the liturgy of the Church is the first authority. Its words conform uneasily to teachers who are ever ready to congratulate us on our aridities.

But the problem is not necessarily just the theoretical one: What importance do we attach to the human experience of the divine? It can be the very practical one: What credence do we give to these particular claims to divine experience? Are not these people (charismatic groups) getting out of their place in claiming spiritual joys, answers to prayer, and other favours such as we would readily concede in the lives of saints and duly accredited holy persons, whose days of prayer and good works have demonstrated their fitness to receive the divine gift? But these are very ordinary people . . . not saints to be sure . . . are they not deceiving themselves?

In fact to suppose that God grants favours to certain people because they are holy is looking at things the wrong way round. We begin to become holy when God – in his gratuitousy love – grants us his favours, and we seek to respond to them. Knowing this, we must surely know also that it is not for us to decide *a priori* whether God has or has not decreed a time in which he scatters new and wonderful graces among his people. We should beware of a possible disbelief founded on the fact that he has not begun with us. But if he has not begun with us, but with some inferior people whom we find it hard to take seriously as recipients of grace, we are also invited. For to be sure we come within the scope of the invitation: 'Come to me, all you who labour and are over burdened, and I will give you rest . . . and you will find rest for your souls' (Matt. 11.28–9, J.B.). These words were not addressed to the cloistered few, nor to especially selected 'great souls'. They are addressed to every man just as he is. They are an invitation at once simple, personal and universal. And Christ reaches out to us, through the sacraments indeed, but also through one another.

If therefore we come into contact with people who claim to have experienced the authenticity of Christ's promise, we should not react by saying: 'Ah! but you are not a saint. That proves you are deceived. May I suggest that you see a psychiatrist?' On the contrary if we meet Christian people who tell us that their lives have been changed radically by

Christ, and that they have discovered in their own experience, that he is their Saviour, redeeming them personally and teaching them by his love, and that now they really want to live for him according to his commandments, we should begin with a willingness to believe that Christ has touched them.

We are entitled to look for some result of his touching, not instant sanctity indeed (what tough judges some of us are!) but some indication that those who claim to be touched by him are more prone to prayer, more concerned about sin, and more sensitive in charity to their neighbours than they were before. We are entitled then to look for the fruits of grace, but not to expect them to be fully ripe because the person feels that they have been changed. And it may be necessary to resist the temptation to suppose that God grants his graces and effects his changes in others in the order that would appeal to us personally. For Christ was always introducing his hearers to the difference between divine attitudes to different situations and the normal human ones.

A priest who finds a charismatic group forming in his parish may ask himself if they are orthodox in their faith. It does not seem that the contrary often occurs, though the possibility of a group going astray must be admitted. More probably he will be asking questions about unconventional behaviour. How does it come that these people get more cheerful before finishing up a lengthy prayer session with a cup of tea than others after drinking a glass of whisky? Have they some secret method of working themselves up, and if so what is it? Moreover if a priest goes to a charismatic meeting and finds some really odd behaviour,* he will sus-

*How extreme joy can struggle with the restraints of a man's cultural heritage is illustrated in H. M. Stanley's *How I found Livingstone*. He had been on a march across Africa for 236 days, and now knew that his journey was to be crowned with success, and that he was on the verge of meeting Livingstone: 'What would I not having given for a bit of friendly wilderness, where, unseen, I might vent my joy in some mad freak, such as idiotically biting my hand, turning a somersault or slashing at trees, in order to allay those excited feelings that were well nigh uncontrollable.'

pect that there is something other than God's inspiration at work here. To judge fairly however, he has to remember that the code of acceptable behaviour for society in a given time and place has no particular validity before God, and that therefore deviations from it are not necessarily wrong or psychopathic. An acute example of this is the so-called gift of tongues: to talk in this way was simply not acceptable behaviour during the first part of this century for the adherents of 'main-line churches'. Let the New Testament say what it would, talking in tongues conflicted with fixed ideas of rational deportment. Whether the Holy Spirit had intended to convey a message that way, or what this gift might have meant in the early Church, was irrelevant. Such persons who enjoyed this gift or were afflicted with this mania, whichever way you looked at it, were to be ejected from the synagogue. And mostly they were. If they did not understand the needs of church order, they had to be. By now I think it is clear that if we demand social conformity, at least we must not ascribe to it a kind of divine right. God has a way of breaking through fixed social patterns for his own purposes – a point frequently illustrated in the Church's history by the lives of the saints. Many saints had to suffer for deviating from normal behaviour, which defined too narrowly how one might serve God without upsetting society. It is true that there are records enough of deluded persons who did the same. Such departures from a social code are inconclusive in themselves from a spiritual point of view. All I want to say here is that God's action is not to be identified with our notions of respectable behaviour; and very often there is such a tendency.

There is too the other side of the matter: an unconscious assumption that a novel behaviour pattern is the key to the reception of divine gifts; or that it is in some way characteristic of the élite. Thus more importance is attached to a way of behaving at a prayer-meeting than to understanding what is really significant. This is a kind of gimmickry. It is also the high road to disaster. There can be some danger of this when the style of a prayer-meeting is lifted or borrowed just as it is from another culture. For in effect whenever a group approaches God in prayer something of our cultural heritage (or somebody else's cultural heritage) enters into its behaviour. In the liturgy itself the cultural sobriety of the Roman Mass distinguishes it from the more suggestively mysterious Eastern rites. This is as it should be. But the danger to which charismatics are exposed is that of imitating the style of other cultural groups (what has been called their 'cultural baggage') and so failing to find the style that is really suitable for their own nation or group. Ironically this can lead to a sort of conformism to what would for a given group be neither natural nor necessary.

Two distinctions are really necessary here. The first is the distinction between renewal, in the broad sense, and charismatic culture or the style of the charismatic meeting. John Richards says rightly: 'It is vital to distinguish between the jewel and its packaging. . . . We need to be sensitive to other Christians who want the jewel without the box or without our particular wrapping paper.'[1]

This is certainly an important point: the 'jewel' is the gift of the Spirit and the reception of the *charismata* that he brings. It is the understanding of this and orientation towards it that distinguishes the charismatic meeting; the style of prayers and hymns and homilies are the 'wrapping'. Growth in personal relationships and mutual love demands a suitable wrapping of some kind as it has to manifest itself, but not necessarily of just one kind. This will lead us to realize that it is up to charismatic groups to develop their own different 'wrapping papers', according to their members' needs. Contemplative nuns will work out for themselves a very different prayer from that encountered at a popular parish level. To quote John Richards again:

Christians for whom silence has always been a crucial

[1] *Renewal,* February, March, 1978

46

activity in their relation to God will be put off renewal if we seem to imply that they must change and engage in verbalised prayer and hearty singing. . . . Many Christians steeped in the Christian music of the centuries will not be attracted to renewal, if it appears to be identified with guitar music and choruses.[2]

Charismatic groups stand to gain enormously by the guidance of the clergy, even as the clergy stand to gain by the outbreak of new spiritual enthusiasm among the laity. Indeed if the clergy hold aloof there is a danger that the prayer groups most in need of guidance are deprived of it in the absence of those best qualified to give it. The qualification does not consist exclusively in having done a sound theological course; nor does ordination in itself constitute a man a readymade spiritual guide. These are presuppositions. It is also a general principal of the spiritual life that to guide others one must have a certain familiarity with the ground to be covered. Obviously in such matters no one person's experience is identical with that of another; it is bound to be limited; priests frequently have to help other persons more advanced than themselves. But they do need to have enough personal experiences of the workings of grace to be able to interpret with its aid, and not merely on the strength of book-learning, what passes in the souls of others.

So then the priest who wants to acquire an informed judgment of charismatics, the graces of which they speak, their problems, and the dangers to which they are exposed, may indeed acquire some part of this knowledge from books or from discussions. There is a fair amount of literature now – though much of it is reportage rather than study. But if he is to exercise the task of guidance, then he does need some experience of the matter himself. And this, one would think, can only be gained by attending charismatic prayer meetings, and, if need be, seeking in all humility for himself renewal in

[2] Ibid.

the Spirit and the gifts that flow from it. Thus he enters into full sympathy with his fellow Christians, who though they are by no means saints (except in St Paul's use of that word), yet are filled with joy and zest for 'the things that are above'.

But he may have another problem. He is the father of the *whole* flock. Piety is nearly always conservative, and for the good reason that we treasure the channels through which we have found grace to flow for us. We treasure, and we seek to preserve intact what we treasure. Hence the priest may ask himself: will he not lose the sympathy, perhaps the support of some of the flock (even the majority?) if he gets involved in some novel form of spirituality? And, if so, would not an attitude of benign but uninvolved tolerance be the best under the circumstances? It is any way much easier to play the part of Gamaliel than that of Paul; less risky too.

This can indeed be a problem. For it is generally true in human affairs, and particularly in spiritual ones, that a move forward – indeed a move anywhere – disturbs some people. But in spiritual affairs it is good people who are most disturbed, because in the nature of the case they are more affected than the indifferent. Every such move begins inevitably in a conservative situation; it can hardly be otherwise.

This problem – that of risking the disturbance of some people – is an ever present one, whenever the Spirit has something new to say to the Churches. Perhaps that was why when the Spirit came 'in the beginning' he manifested his presence so dramatically by causing the Apostles and those they baptised to break out into the strange speech we call glossolalia, 'tongues'. For even at that time this was an odd phenomenon, and it still brings a 'Why that?' to the lips of many Christians. It may be that without disturbing us in some way the Holy Spirit cannot proceed, for we tend to bring religion down to the level of our own normal life: He says 'No! see I am other, I am different!' and we are thrown into disorder by the discovery. This is a speculative thought, but it is certain enough that every new tide of grace in the history of the Church runs into opposition before it is recognised for what it is. Historically almost any religious order that represented a breakaway from the accepted social pattern (a pattern in which religion had in fact an *allowed* place) ran into this.

What is novel in the present situation (or so it seems) is the sudden and astonishing spread of personal awareness of Jesus the Saviour among perfectly ordinary people. If they could all be classed as the religious type known as *exaltés, illuminati,* that might explain it; if they could all be written off as neurotics in search of a cure, that would explain it. But they are not at all persons of one kind or temperament or standard of intelligence. Yet they all declare a new joy in Jesus; they all unstiffen and seek to carry the love of Christ to others. Is not this a phenomenon for which we should give thanks on our knees? Does it not conform admirably with the Gospel promise: 'Know that I am with you always, yes to the end of time' (Matt. 28.20 J.B.)? This was not a promise reserved to the Apostles, but a promise for all his followers.

There may be a tendency in some clerical circles to look suspiciously at any new outbreak of fervour as more likely to be a pathetic illusion than a true stirring of grace. It is not difficult to pick such cases out of the pages of history, and presume that this must be the same thing. On the other hand, is there no danger in accepting morosely and unquestioningly the simple fact of thousands or millions of cases of lapsing from religion, as if these persons did not in themselves demonstrate a sad and sick situation calling aloud for a new tonic from God's hand? It is as if we were more alert to the dangers to be encountered in a lively and vivacious street than to those of a city in which thousands were quietly dying of plague. The latter may seem a more tranquil kind of place, but is the wrong kind of tranquillity.

A priest is a man conscious of his position of responsibility. Others have responsibilities too for different aspects of our welfare; indeed in a society such as ours, we are nearly all locked together in some form of responsibility for one another's welfare. And the priest's responsibility, being for souls, is really the heaviest one. It is not discharged by the merely routine accomplishment of his duties, for he is responsible for showing Christ to others, and that demands an inward growth in Christ quite distinct from the actual duties he performs; it is what gives success and reality to those duties. Moreover he is aware that he represents the caring Christ, who is not indifferent to poor Christians because they are indifferent to him. Those who are indifferent to the Christ in whose name they have been baptised are in fact legion. How heavy then is the priest's responsibility for doing all he can that they may be saved!

If then there is given to the world today a new spiritual force, functioning with the approval of the Church's authority, claiming to be a channel through which God's latest gifts for the renewal of souls are exuberantly passing, can he remain indifferent to such a claim? Suspicious he may be. . . . Grounds for doubt he may have. . . . A given situation may present special difficulties. . . . But indifferent he can hardly be. For in the present state of the Church and of the world, far too much is at stake.

3 The Religious Life and the Charismatic Movement

A Spanish lady once said to me: 'I understand perfectly well how valuable the charismatic movement is to us laity who are a nothing, but what use can it be to all those dedicated persons over there in the monastery who already spend their time in long hours of prayer?' Many persons, without subscribing to her description of the laity, or to her uncomplicated reverence for monastic life, would still agree that the question is a significant one. In fact many religious, both men and women, enclosed and active, are involved in the charismatic movement. A fair-sized charismatic meeting usually shows a relatively high proportion of religious sisters; and a prayer group is frequently to be found in monasteries of enclosed monks or nuns. However it is rare at present for all or even the majority of a religious community to be involved. This can cause problems. If Sister X speaks in tongues and Mother Superior disapproves of the whole business, we are, at any rate on the verge of a problem. But apart from this the lady's question calls for an answer; and it is not the only question concerning the religious life either.

Religious grow up with the understanding that their Holy Rule delineates for them personally the form that the service of God takes in their lives. (I use the word 'Holy Rule' to cover whatever documents set out the special way of life each Institute has.) Everyone is dependent on the Gospel, and the Gospel is illustrated and expounded by a whole range of spiritual works, which are the product of the Church's life. But to the Holy Rule is ascribed a special function; it is the specific code detailing how a religious in his or her personal life is to behave; it is an interpretation of the Gospel in practical terms, such as to enable the religious to move forward to the fulfilment of Christ's command: Be ye perfect as your heavenly Father is perfect (Matt. 5.48, Douai). And for this purpose (apart from the specific aim of the Institute) it gives a specific shape to the Gospel message, and forms a number of individuals into a well-knit community. It has been composed in the first place by an exceptionally gifted servant of God, the founder or the foundress, and it has the approval of the highest authority of the Church. It has also normally the weight of the authority that is acquired through years of experience.

How then does a religious whose feet have been planted on a safe road to holiness suddenly become ecstatic (for they do) about something else? What need have they of anything more? Is not a transference of ideal involved here, and is not such a transference likely to end in shipwreck? This objection is substantial, and its weight is likely to be felt as much by the religious who describe themselves as charismatic as by those who do not.

The objection might be formulated thus: 'Our form of religious life is our charism; we don't need anything fresh.' The first part of this sentence is basically true, but it does draw attention to the fact that the word *charism* is used in various quite different ways. Basically it always means a gift of the Holy Spirit, but then how various in kind are his gifts! Pope Paul VI used the word very frequently, but with a variety of connotations.[1] Sometimes it is used (as in the sentence under discussion) for a special kind of inspiration, a call to live in a certain way. In this sense we use it of prophets and of founders of religious orders, (and their followers) in whom we recognise that they have by their way of life something distinctive (maybe something challenging) to say. But sometimes the word is used of gifts given

---

[1] Edward O'Connor C.S.C.: *Pope Paul and the Spirit* pp. 245–6

specifically for the benefit of others, belonging however to the very structure of the Church. We might thus speak of the charism of the priesthood or the episcopate, with which would be associated accompanying gifts necessary for the full use of the essential one (for example: discernment in their hierarchy, evangelism in the priest). Obviously this is quite a different meaning. Again we speak of a charism as of a supernatural gift of an extraordinary or miraculous nature, as are the gifts of tongues or the healing ministries. And finally we should note the sense which Cardinal Suenens employs when he says: 'There is no such thing as a non-charismatic Christian.'[2] For we are all gifted by the Holy Spirit in our baptism; what is at issue is the development that proceeds from the initial giving.

Since the words *charism* and its derivative *charismatic* are so rich in meanings, and these meanings differ so widely, and are yet held together by a certain radical unity, it is not surprising that the present lively debate runs into the danger of some confusion.

What then is it precisely that distinguishes the battling charismatic whom we associate with the Movement from others who also enjoy the gifts of the Spirit? It is not that they belong to any one class, be it clerical, religious or lay; nor that they are of any one temperament be it lively or sedate, impetuous or slow-moving; nor are they an élite nor a separate structure of any kind. What modern charismatics propound as distinguishing marks are (or at any rate include):

1.   That the baptismal grace has been renewed in them with marked effects.

2.   That there are certain gifts of the Spirit towards which modern Christians are simply not orientated, and that this part of the New Testament teaching calls for resuscitation.

3.   That Christ's promise ('If two of you on earth agree to ask anything at all it will be granted to you by my Father in Heaven. For where two or three meet in my name, I shall

[2] Cardinal Suenens: *Your God?* p. 93

53

be there with them' (Matt. 18.19, J.B.)) means that Christ will manifest his power as an everyday reality – and not merely as a reward for high sanctity.

So that the objection that the religious life is in itself a charism and that nothing fresh is needed contains a very real truth but is also misleading. For we all stand in need of a fresh effusion of the Spirit, and should desire it intensely; and new effusions bring new gifts or new *charisms* as the Spirit wills.

The religious life is the result of a gift of grace, following which an individual gives himself or herself to be led to serve God in a specific way. It has been said that the charism (special gift of grace) of the early monks was prayer. An immense thirst for prayer led men first into deserts, and then into communities to answer their call. Likewise the great Franciscan movement was a highly charismatic phenomenon recalling the simplicity of the first preaching of the Gospel. And every founder has been touched by the grace of a special call to meet either some human need or God-given spiritual desire. God blessed them, manifesting that it was his work in the quantity and quality of their followers. They felt themselves called in person. And so for their followers, to lead the life means a special renunciation of self, and a surrender of one's future to God; in their vows they show their commitment to his leading.

Now we live in an age of renewal. The inference is that to religious the Holy Spirit offers a new infusion of the graces that they need to lead their life in joyous fulfilment. This is something that most of us do need afresh; in fact we are always needing that something fresh, that we call new fervour, some of us more, some of us less. Renewal of heart concerns religious at least as much as any one else; it enables them to make fuller use of their charism, maybe to understand it better; but that is not to *add* to it. It renews it as one stirs up a fire.

But does that imply involvement in a charismatic movement that has begun as, and largely still is, a movement of the laity? Only in the sense explained in the last chapter. The Holy Spirit works through this channel and in it he shows what gifts he has to offer the Church in our day. Because it is a renewal of spiritual life and not a novelty and because it is a channel of actual giving, it is something of concern especially to those whose lives are already a response to a special gift of grace. For where grace is concerned we are always in need of what the Spirit offers anew.

Hence the appeal of the charismatic movement to religious. Hence also the tension. It is easier for an individual to say 'I need spiritual renewal' than it is for a whole Institute. There is however, no betrayal of the grace that already flourishes in an Institute, in desiring an infusion of new fire.

It should be observed then that the religious does not through the charismatic grace receive a new ideal, so much as an understanding of what he or she is trying to be already; and with this understanding a new ease in it. The Holy Spirit is in this matter the life-giver, of whose touch we are always in need. Those who are conscious of being renewed in heart become more conscious also of certain things that effect deeply the dedication which they have wanted to make of themselves: the personal love for them which Jesus showed in calling them to his special service; the nearness of his presence; his love for their brothers or sisters in religion; the depth of his past favours to them; ways in which they can serve him more lovingly; the recognition that their past service has been inadequate in some ways . . . and much more. None of this enlightenment is going to conflict with their already received religious ideal; on the contrary it will bring it out, as a good light makes the beauty of a work of art more clear. The first essential point is then that the grace of renewal does not lead to a breaking away from the religious life but to fulfilment in it. This is just as true for the religious involved in the charismatic movement as it is for other vocations in life. The normal rule and expectation is this: that as the housewife becomes a better housewife through the new grace she receives, and as the priest becomes a move effective priest in his own sphere, so the grace of the effusion of the spirit works inside the state to which the religious is called and not away from it. Any other principle would be very suspect indeed. However it must also be said that this single general principle does not cover all cases; this will be discussed on a later page of this chapter.

Certain reservations may occur to religious, especially religious superiors, when they ask themselves whether they should become involved in the movement. What does it add to a system of spirituality that is complete already, and not only to a system of spirituality, but to all those facilities and arrangements for a devout life which every institute offers its followers? Is any new form of spirituality called for? The answer as already indicated is: that essentially, no new form of spirituality is called for; it is not about that, but about the acceptance of new graces of priceless value which the Spirit offers to the Church today. Can these graces be found only in the charismatic movement? No one should assert that. One can only say that great graces are received through it, and, that of those involved in it, some persons seem to have a special ministry for communicating the grace of renewal, and other things such as interior or even physical healing as well. Christianity is essentially an event, and the spread of renewal is essentially an event in its history. It does not add precisely; it is the means of bringing to life. And since human beings are in the end but human, the possession of the most perfect spiritual teaching is not the same as being fully alive to it; we *always* need more abundant life of the kind that Christ came to bring.

Certainly there will be differences between religious and laity in their angle of approach. For many laity the weekly prayer meeting is an outstanding event in their week because they have no other occasions for joint prayer; whereas religious pray together several times every day. Moreover the laity begin to experience the meaning of community life as a Christian ideal through the development of the prayer group; but the religious already has a very definite formation

56

making him (or her) part of a community; and it is also true that while for many lay people the holiness of other persons is something first glimpsed through prayer meetings, most religious have the benefit of a tradition that has brought them into contact with persons who have attained a degree of holiness. From these points of view then the religious and the lay person approach the charismatic experience from very different angles. This, if one may so put it, is no problem to the Spirit of God, who knows what each of us need, but it does call for clear thinking on the part of those who expect new grace, as to what exactly they are expecting. The same grace of renewal surely, and share of the gifts of the Spirit too, but according to their own needs and the services they are called on to render.

Are not the gifts of the Spirit found to be divisive? Do they not inevitably lead to the creation of more new problems than to the solution of old ones? For example: if a very living experience of prayer is found only in the meetings of a specific prayer-group, it may build up a sense that that group is in fact a more meaningful community than one's own religious community. This means that the religious community involved may well feel threatened. Moreover in practice a religious may get caught up in what is going on at so many levels in the renewal movement as to lose balance, or overdo things physically, accept engagements beyond what he (she) can cope with, and this is to the real detriment of his (her) religious commitment. It is of course not only religious who can find themselves exposed to this danger: in their own context fathers and mothers of families have to have regard to their prior commitments.

Such problems can be complicated by the faults of religious, who although receiving such gifts, show a lack of obedience, indifference to community prayer, lack of humility. And therefore there lies a grave responsibility on any religious to whom special gifts have been granted, to labour the harder to give edification to all by the practice of the basic Christian virtues. Indeed if they do not do this, their work becomes ambivalent – they help some by their gifts, deter others by their faults.

Deeper than the practical problems that can arise around a highly gifted member of the community, is the question of élitism. Let us suppose that some members of a community call themselves 'charismatic' and claim to be the recipients of new gifts of the Spirit, but the bulk of the community care for none of these things. Are not the charismatic group liable to a charge of élitism? How do they escape the dilemma: either you claim to have entered on a new plane of spiritual life – which is serious and challenging – or you are merely engaged in a new style of prayer which happens to appeal to you, but is not in itself particularly important?

It seems to me that a person is liable to a charge of élitism if they feel themselves better than others. And 'charismatics' cannot deny that they claim a spiritual awareness and fruits from it which they had not known previously, and that they believe that most of the other persons with whom they live would benefit from these things. But this is a long way from thinking that one is a better servant of God than another, or rendering more valuable service. The 'charismatic' believes in his heart that he has undergone a deep transformation in his personality, altering his previous interior state to his present one, and that therefore he is a better person than he was. But this does not mean that he is a better person than another person or has corresponded to grace more faithfully than another. And if he wishes in his heart that the same kind of grace be given to another person it is not that the other may come up to his standard, but that they may receive an increase of divine indwelling, making them yet happier, more joyful, more alive in the Lord than they are now.

This then does not mean at all that he writes them down as less meritorious than himself. Indeed his own renewal works in precisely the opposition direction. For essential to it is the grace of *metanoia* or repentance. He knows now as never before the enormity of his debt to God, the gratuitousness of the grace to him, his own sad record of neglected grace, the ugliness of his past sins . . . he cries with the psalmist:

My offences truly I know them;
My sin is always before me (Ps. 50.5 Grail).

It would be an intolerable burden but for the warm, enfolding love of Jesus, and the astonishing sense of new birth in him, and the knowledge that God's sure plan is to lead him steadily onwards to the fulfilment of every capacity for joy. For this reason this world too is full of new beauty for him and he feels enriched by God at every level. He cannot but want to share these experiences with others, for joy shared is joy doubled. But this does not make him feel superior to others; it does fill him with astonishment at God's goodness to himself a sinner; his sin is always before him.

I have known it suggested that to avoid the danger of divisiveness, *all* or *none* in a community should be involved in the charismatic movement. However this well meant suggestion seems to be based on pure ignorance. Since: (1) No one can renew another spiritually or grant him charismatic gifts. It is not some automatic procedure but a gift of the Spirit, who gives as *he* wishes. (2) No one can make another even want to be changed. Fundamentally a lot of people do not want to be changed. They would accept an improved version of themselves (something in the style of a portrait that flatters), but for those deep personality changes that the Holy Spirit works in us they have no desire at all, nor any suspicion that they need them. (3) Religious communities (as they well know) are not composed in order to impose a uniform mediocrity on their members. It is impossible for a conscientious superior to say that if X is indifferent to renewal, therefore Y cannot be permitted to seek it either. Obedience is not intended to hinder the path of grace for one lest they out distance another.

In general renewal of all kinds goes on in the Church

59

today. And as was said in Chapter I, personal renewal is most necessary, and is often effected through the instrumentality of the Charismatic Movement. But it cannot be imposed. In many cases a community has to come to a gradual understanding of what is being offered (the essential things) and so prepare itself by those mysterious thought processes known to communities, but which cannot be rushed.

What about the question of the unsatisfactory religious who claims to be 'charismatic'. To use the terminology of my own order, what if Fr Abbot has a 'charismatic' monk who is not particularly edifying or self-sacrificing?; or is notably self-willed?; or is just a foolish person? The Abbot, if this is his first contact with a person claiming to be 'charismatic' will inevitably think critically of the movement, and regard claims made for it as of doubtful value. But it would be equally logical to think critically of the monastic life. For the man in question was formed as a monk first, but the formation has not been a success. If then he receives or thinks he has received the charismatic grace at a later stage it falls on one who has had a faulty formation. Graces vary in the depth at which they effect us; if this monk's grace is a deep one, it will certainly involve *metanoia* or repentance. It should help him to grasp where he stands, and what manner of life he is leading. But it may be that he receives an initial grace, something that brings him to life so to speak, but does not as yet touch the depths. Such things happen. Not all graces are equally decisive. If this should be the case the man may need some one to help him to make new choices. And if his Abbot is experienced in the ways of renewal, he will be well placed to help him. It is a reason why superiors, even if they feel no personal need, stand to gain by exploring personally this new source of grace. Indeed superiors cannot afford to be ignorant of new sources of graces, of which their subjects may be in need.

It seems also to be a fact of experience that the Spirit of God can fall upon a person who is psychologically immature.

It is not necessary to speak of spiritual immaturity since we are all spiritually immature from God's point of view – that is to say we are persons whose comprehension of divine things is just about beginning to show signs of dawning. But some of us are more psychologically immature than their life calls for. As far as one can see the Spirit grants graces and gifts to those who are open to them in great abundance but not always in the order which we in our human prudence would have selected ourselves. Thus St Paul congratulated the Corinthians on not being 'lacking in any spiritual gift' and yet told them that they were infants (*nepioi*) in Christ (I Cor. 3. 1–2 R.S.V.), and not ready for 'solid food'. He was himself no doubt the channel through which the spiritual gifts had come, and there is no implication that things had been done the wrong way around, or that there should have been no conferring of spiritual gifts until the Corinthians had grown up to be mature and responsible Christians.[3] The same kind of thing can happen today. The fact that a man may be in need of greater maturity does not invalidate other gifts that the Spirit may have for him. Gifts no doubt are given to encourage, to lead on, to build up, or edify, but a marked need for psychological maturity is more likely to be met by a steady flow of grace than an immediate miracle. Meanwhile other gifts demonstrate that God is at work, and remind us not to impose too human a judgment, for God is not obliged to do things our way. We learn to lay our deepest needs before him and also those of others; but we do not impose on him how he shall reply. That in itself would be the sign of immaturity.

We have touched on a number of apprehensions that may affect religious confronted with the Charismatic Movement: there is the fear of being asked to accept a devaluation of all that has previously made up one's life, or of the rules of the

---

[3] cf. his attitude to the Galatians who 'began with the Spirit' and then went back to reliance on the works of the Law (3.3).

Institute itself,★ or of accepted forms of piety; there is the fear of divisiveness in the community; or of simply not knowing how to incorporate an unexpected new grace into the shape of our actual life. There is also another kind of fear: it is a more deeply hidden one. This is the fear of the numinous. It may seem strange to refer to this in connection with persons whose lives are directed to the service of God, and who sincerely desire to converse with him. Yet as the Israelites knew of old, divine power is a tremendous, an awe-ful thing. If we feel it around it causes awe, and some persons, not necessarily unspiritual ones, have a fear lest they feel it around. They would rather not; they do not know how it will affect them; it is unpredictable in its 'otherness'. The Israelites in their fears at Mount Sinai said to Moses: 'Let the Lord speak to you only, and not to us directly' (cf. Exod. 20.18). So we may likewise feel: Let the Lord in his intercourse with us, confine himself to the normal channels; we don't want to feel his power. This puts it rather crudely, but in substance many persons have this unwillingness, due to fear of God's power, deep down in them. And hence it is difficult for them to yield beyond the point of feeling in control of the situation. The remedy is to accept him at his word: He says that he is all Love. But for this fact indeed he would be terrible in his slightest manifestation. But essentially what he wants to manifest is his love. The message is the message of the prophet Hosea: 'I will betroth you to myself forever betroth you with integrity and justice, with tenderness and love; I will betroth you to myself with faithfulness, And you will come to know Yahweh' (Hosea 2.21-2, J.B.).

This betrothal was fulfilled through the Incarnation. As we read how it came about we must be struck by the number of times 'Fear not!' is said to those who are called to play a

---

★We prescind here entirely from the work of the evaluation for modern use of the rules of religious institutes that is going on through General Chapters. This official reconsideration is of course another aspect of the general renewal of the Church.

part in the mystery of God's intervention in human affairs (Luke 1.13, 30; Mark 6.50; Matt. 28.5, 10; cf. Mark 9.6). For, as it turns out, it is this same God, whose power inspires dread if we so much as sense its presence, who is the antidote to all fear. He teaches us in practice:

> Do not be afraid, for I have redeemed you;
> I have called you by your name, you are mine. (Isa. 43.1, J.B.)

It is an individual lesson that he gives, even as he did to a dejected Paul at Corinth: 'Do not be afraid. I am with you' (Acts 18.9, 10, J.B.).

Have we perhaps less worthy fears? Fears of the demands on us that may follow a surrender to this tremendous love? We have desired him, yes. But now that he is actually at the gate, we are hesitant about getting up to open the door to his invading presence. It wants thinking over carefully. . . !

Or fears, too human, but very human nevertheless, simply of being disapproved of by others whom we esteem? It is easy to say that we should not be concerned with human respect; but in fact we are and should be intimately concerned with one another. Our reputation is the last of our personal goods, and one which we do not part with readily, and never without a secret hope of recovering it later.

Some gifts of the Spirit are not, it seems good for our reputation in the present climate. 'Away with him! He speaks Latin!' said Jack Cade of the Archbishop (Henry VI, Part III). 'Away with her! She speaks in tongues', might be a modern equivalent. It was all very well for the Corinthians; they were near enough to the day of Pentecost for their tongue-speaking to be seen as a normal Christian phenomenon. But that doesn't apply to us now. Today we are called on to find reasons for such a thing happening now; to say that it is a gift of the Holy Spirit (cf. St Luke or St Paul) is not usually considered an adequate answer. What obviously delighted St Luke and called for St Paul's careful teaching, positively scares some modern Christians, who find it extremely difficult to believe that the Holy Spirit should be doing something so irrational as to renew the state of affairs after Pentecost.

The vow of obedience can in certain circumstances, give rise to tension. For example the case can occur in which religious who have become involved in the Charismatic Movement find that their activities are not much approved of by their superior. It should not be assumed at all that a superior who *is* involved will approve of such activities, while one who is *not* involved is going to disapprove; the difference is that the former's judgment will be based on a personal knowledge of what is at stake. In fact most superiors, involved or not, are sympathetic to this new resurgence of spiritual life, since their job is easy, hard or impossible according to the condition of those over whom they are placed.

An unhappy religious is by no means necessarily an unsatisfactory religious – but nevertheless such a one has a problem of a very deep kind. And it is the business of the superior to help if possible. So that if there is a possibility of solution through the Charismatic Movement, this is of importance to both parties. It is not at this level that difficulty occurs. But a clash can arise between the requirements of the religious life and an intense engagement in a charismatic programme. We use the word 'programme' deliberately for it is here that the difficulty most easily arises – not, that is, in the grace of renewal, but in the activities that follow from receiving exceptional new gifts of the Spirit. And who shall say No to them? Are not such happenings one of the marks by which the Kingdom of Christ is to be recognised? (Matt. 10.7). Yet at some point or other, it is likely that the superior's permission will be necessary, and he or she, by virtue of their office, thinks in terms of the good of other members of the community or of the requirements of general good order.

And in the event of a clash occurring between 'the divine

will' as seen through the voice of authority invested in the religious superior, and the 'divine will' as apparently inviting to a ministry of great value to the Church as a whole – what then?

It is no doubt beyond the scope of a writer to decide what should happen in individual cases. But the general principle must surely be that the religious follows the path of obedience to which he is vowed, and that God will provide otherwise if he wills. After all God, we believe, first called the religious to that great act of confidence in him which is the vow of obedience, and therefore he will see him through to the end of the matter. This seems to be the pattern inculcated by the saints. That most charismatic of saints, Catharine of Siena, has left it on record that while she did not always understand clearly what the Holy Spirit was saying to her, yet she always knew exactly what her superiors were saying to her. Nor is there any lack of such examples. St Simon Stylites had a most unusual vocation: he spent his whole life praying on the top of a pillar. From there he exercised an astonishing and widespread ministry. However, not surprisingly, this odd form of Christianity came in for criticism. So he was ordered by ecclesiastical authority to come down. No sooner did he hear these words ordering him to abandon his chosen way of life, than he was on his way down to earth. By this prompt action the authorities were convinced of his authentic spirituality, and he was told to go back again.

Yet saints too have been known to change their state in order to fulfil what they believed to be a divine call. St Antony of Padua was an Augustinian Canon for ten years, and then became a friar minor in order to seek martyrdom in Morocco. It turned out that that was not the divine will for him either, and he ended up, quite unexpectedly to himself, as a celebrated preacher in France and Italy. His story shows us that to some God manifests his will in stages, not always those anticipated by canon law or foreseeable by human planning; to follow it is the only ultimate rule.

However, we are not all saints nor all gifted with special ministries. It is when my small ministry is hindered or suppressed that I am hurt, and perplexed too; hurt, because it gave me joy, perplexed because only God could have given it to me . . . and what right has the superior to impede the workings of grace through me? Put in this crude way, the problem may be relatively rare, but there will be some such cases. It is not necessarily a case of ecclesiastical authority versus individual charism, for discernment is a charism appropriate to a superior, and he may be exercising it appropriately.

In general, I think, we come back to this: obedience is the general law and God will be more glorified by its practice and the benefits entailed than by revolt against it or withdrawal from it. This is not to deny that there may be special cases in which a religious feels sure that God is saying something new to him; such cases seem to call for special guidance as apart from one's own interior promptings or exterior success. But there seems no reason to depart from the normal teaching that simple obedience and trust in God's Providence to bring all things to his greater glory lie at the heart of the process by which God makes his saints, and fits them for his purposes.

And on the other side it is surely true that if superiors have a duty to promote and make use of the natural talents of members of their institute, they will have no less a duty to encourage them in the use of new gifts, if God gives them such.

Finally, there are without doubt special and extraordinary ministries. While there is a natural tendency to suppose that God gives such ministries only to persons of special and extraordinary sanctity, this does not seem to be borne out by the evidence. God gives as he wills. In such cases their superiors will recognize that God is doing something special, and will readily give scope for it. This may cause inconvenience, since religious rules are not written for such cases, but evidently they emerge, and call for recognition.

In some Institutes the fact that some, and some only of the sisters go out to attend charismatic prayer meetings causes some tension. 'No one minds', said a sister to me, 'if we want to go out to entertainment; it's when we want to go to a prayer-meeting that they feel hurt.' The implications of this sentence want weighing.

When a small group of religious want to meet *inside* their own house to pray, there is not usually much tension, but there is sometimes mystification – or even scepticism – especially if the group cannot explain very clearly what they hope for. Their own conversion? The conversion of others? Special spiritual favours, only to be found by a special kind of prayer? None of these answers, nor all together seems quite adequate. Yet the group does seek personal renewal, not as just an accomplished fact but as on on-going process. It does believe that a certain style of prayer is often a door towards this, and that shared prayer is an instrument by which we learn to love one another at a deeper level, and that this is something learnt through practice. It does hope for the gifts of the Spirit that follow renewal. It does develop a zeal in praying for the community and a sense of its needs, and a desire that God may grant his gifts more abundantly to others. The kind of gifts that are of most significance here are those which help others, that build up a community, that break down fears, those that remove long-standing traumata and help to overcome personal antipathies, or that increase true discernment or the capacity for counselling. What is important is that the group learns to follow the leading of the Spirit, to desire what he knows them to need, and not be intent on any programme of its own.

If there are certain problems specific to the religious life, it is also true that the religious life confers certain advantages, and its members stand to reap accordingly. Let us consider these next.

The first of these advantages is that every religious has a training in the ascetic life, and is taught to accept discipline as part of his or her approach to God. By discipline here we do not mean specifically the regulations imposed by the Institute, but the knowledge and the habit of putting to use the knowledge that there is a certain order to be imposed on our disordered nature as we venture to approach God. And that this remains so however good God is to us. To be aware of the touch of God is not the same thing as to be cured of one's defects; to enjoy the divine sweetness does not prove that one is selfless.

Every religious learns that humility is basic in the spiritual life, and that this humility is not a private understanding between ourselves and Almighty God, but something to be translated into every action of daily life.

By tradition too every religious learns (or used to learn) that obedience to a human superior is a safeguard against our most deeply rooted enemy, our self-will. It is so easy to decide that what is good for ourselves is God's will; and this is so near the truth that it is difficult for an individual to distinguish between what is deeply good and what seems to be so.

Every religious learns the difference between feeling uplift in prayer and getting out of bed in the morning to pray.

Likewise religious know the difference between proclaiming the beauty of charity, queen of the virtues, and actually setting oneself to serve one's neighbour. And still more perhaps, the difference between teaching or preaching love of one's neighbours and combating one's personal human dislikes.

In brief a religious knows from experience the difference between accepting with joy all that God gives, and bringing our humble offering of service, of self-immolation and self-correction to lay at his feet.

It is in the combination of these two things that the way of holiness lies.

And therefore the religious who has been trained to set about the task of overcoming himself or herself, knows someting indispensable for the putting of God's pentecostal gifts to profit. Others of course need this knowledge too;

they may have it since spiritual training is not confined to religious, or they may yet have to come to it. But without it, the Spirit will be infused in vain, and however wonderful a person's experiences may be, the end result will not be spiritual progress. The advantage of the religious then consists in this: Firstly, their whole training is a basis for the reception of the Spirit. What will come to them as new will be a new *experience* of the loving kindness of God, corresponding to, or better, surpassing, all that they have been trained to expect. It will quicken to life their ascetic training, even as their ascetic training safeguards them from thinking that the growth in the life of the Spirit is compatible with a self-indulgent way of living.

Secondly: we normally say that the experience of renewal implies a new relationship with Christ, whether that is marked by some 'summit' experience, or is the result of a steady growth, the significance of which only becomes clear after a certain time. Now for such an experience religious profession is a spring-board. Every religious has from the start accepted a need for an increase in his relationship with Christ. This is at the very heart of the religious life. Without a *living* relationship of this kind, the religious life will be a disaster, or at best a half-human life, from which much is excluded and little gained. In fact since religious are human, their bond with Christ can vary in strength and depth, and so they will reflect according to their state – vitality or torpor, joyousness or gloom. But however they are, and whoever they are, whatever speeds up the process to which they are vowed can only be good news. It is not a new end that is sought; nor a new master; nor even that we should claim an infallible technique for entering into closer touch with that Master. All we can say (and it is much) is that Christ draws his own towards himself in a new outburst of love in our world today, and that to profit by this divine action, the religious has, if he will use it, a personal basic orientation through the act of his profession.

The third advantage of religious in seeking renewal concerns community life. It is well known that a prayer-group, indeed any form of shared prayer-group, tends to develop the instinct for community in its members. This is because there grows in it a sense of being the Mystical Body of Christ; an inner reality that calls for outward demonstration in loving service to one another. The wider extension of this sense may lead to certain problems for religious who already belong to a community, and indeed a community calling for total involvement. That such problems are met and have to be reckoned with, should not hide the wider truth: religious as persons already living in community, and persons who have a considerable experience of the actualities of community life, are one ahead of persons who have not yet a community at all. The problem of the latter is that of creating a community; the problem of the former is that of adjustment, of learning how to bring the gifts of the Spirit to bear on their community life to the enrichment of all. Their down-to-earth practical knowledge tells them the problems; they are in a position to go on from there, not only with more joyful hearts, but with new gifts or increased ones, at the service of those whom they live.

What profit exactly may a community of religious persons hope to draw from the involvement of its members in this movement for renewal in the Spirit?

In the first place it is true of such a community that it gains and loses, is happy or sad, through the interior state of its individual members, and more acutely so than a prayer-group of lay persons. In other words the gains of an individual affect the general good even more closely than in a more loosely knit organism. Let us consider some examples of this general principle.

There is the case of the religious who gets 'stuck' in his or her spiritual evolution. So indeed may we all; but in a religious community if one member gets 'stuck' this, owing to the common life, is going to mean a loss for all. The occasions religious have for edifying or disconcerting one another are more numerous and more intimate, than for persons less closely connected. If then there is a means through which such a one may be 'unfrozen' and released from their personal predicament (and this may amount to the setting in motion of a whole log-jam of personal problems) this will bring benefit to the whole community. The grace given to one warms the hearts of all.

Another aspect is this: the theory of the religious life supposes that those who follow it are happy people, whose natures are well-balanced and rich enough to support the burden of additional sacrifices. But if they are not this, they carry a heavier burden than was ever intended. Nor is it always true that generous resolves and efforts overcome the interior weights of a depressive nature. Mostly I think religious are happy people. But certainly there are some who are not happy persons (this does not mean that they are just grumblers or ungenerous); there are no statistics, and happiness is a relative quality anyway. But certainly there are religious who either from a depressive nature, or a genuinely distressing situation, or from some form of emotional starvation, have parted company with joy over a long time. Even on the human level, they have not had a good laugh for years. This is not necessarily the *direct* result of the religious life, but goes with unfulfilledness. They may have thought that the religious life would bring them a happiness they had not known before (was not that expected?) and it has not happened. Or indeed in some way their religious life may have gone sour on them. Either way, unhappiness in the heart is for them like nitrogen in the lungs of a long-distance runner. It produces a permanent sense of fatigue.

What price the grace that alters this condition? What is it worth to the individual – and to the community?

A word of caution however may be in place here. There have been plenty of persons who have received such a grace in the very course of being prayed over, or immediately afterwards, for example waking up to it in the night. They have received it instantaneously, explosively, to their utter astonishment. They have known that for them it has been

71

every bit as striking a manifestation of divine power as if they had been healed of a deep physical wound. Such stories get printed, or otherwise circulated. Such phenomena are however probably the rarer ones. More often when a deep psychological change is called for, it takes place more slowly over weeks or months, and the person is called on to co-operate in his own healing. If he makes no such effort or even clings to old attitudes unconformable to the personality he has elected to be, then the work of the Spirit will be hindered. Joy may be but a spark at first barely distinguishable from hope; there has to be a surrender to the new *confidence* and a grasping of the new birth of *faith* that grow as from seedlings in the soul.

Another trouble to which renewal in the Spirit is the answer is that of those 'hang-ups' which occur between two individuals. A 'hang-up' is a situation of non-communication, almost of excommunication, into which individuals fall as into a pit from which they cannot get out. Between such persons intercourse is confined to the strictly necessary; there is no geniality in their meeting, still less any exchange of love. They would not admit that they cordially disliked one another, for the 'hang-up' is essentially an unresolved situation; so they live side by side; both intend to keep their rule but neither succeeds, for the law of love has defeated them, and they can only keep up the appearances. Perhaps each sees the other as a 'personal cross' but not the kind of cross you embrace. The situation is mildly scandalous to other members of the community; sometimes one should delete *mildly* from this assessment. No one knows how to alter this painful situation.

And it is not so uncommon, nor necessarily confined to religious communities. It can occur equally well in a family relationship. Once it has taken root even the separation of the persons, the passage of years, even the death of one of the persons, does not cure the wound, nor unbind a person so bound. It is beyond the power of those caught up in the situation to deal with. Of course not all such troubles are equally deep – they vary from an antipathy indulged in till it has gained control to a deepset bitterness arising out of what was felt as an irreparable wrong.

To say that the grace needed may come through the renewal is inadequate; it *must* come, or there can be no renewal. And it comes through one of those graces that pierce the heart, bringing about deep personality changes. Nor can one do more than suggest the nature of the grace, for it is highly personal and individual. It may come as a strong pressure on the will, or as a shaft of repentance direct from Calvary, or as some fresh vision of another human being. After all if I see a person, any person, with the loving tenderness with which Christ sees them, will not that be a totally different vision from the one that I normally have? And Christ sees them from the first moment of their conception, through the circumstances that have made them as they are; and he sustains them in every moment of their life until the time, when, all defect removed, he receives them as his own redeemed brother into his kingdom, where they will be an example of his victory and a source of his joy throughout eternity. We cannot give ourselves even the beginning of this insight. But the Lord can give such an insight to us; at the cost perhaps of personality changes in us. Then only can one fulfil his commandment: To love in the way that he loved.

One does not need to consider only the question of individual estrangements to perceive how much room for progress there may be. It is not only minor 'thorns of scandal' that should be plucked out; there is room also for a collective advance in the love of the brotherhood. Community life is of necessity a sensitive thing. We are each of us sensitive as to where we stand in the estimation of others. This, combined with various precepts of a rather negative kind where personal relationships are concerned, can lead to a community life in which there is little real openness between persons. It is a common source of poverty in communities, perhaps one not sufficiently attended to, that the members lack confidence in one another. The laity indeed may speak highly of the help and understanding that they have received from these religious, but somehow they do not communicate to each other the warmth and strength and the help that comes from mutual confidence, or only in a rather restricted way. This may be because, for all their living closely together, they only know one another from outside or on a level that is not the deepest. In fact the deepest level of knowing one another is reached through shared prayer. Nothing draws persons together in a strengthening unity so much as a sharing of graces through the act of prayer. In general sharing is the principle of unity; the question is: How far do we go? No doubt in earlier ages the Divine Office was less formal in monasteries than it is now. Praying aloud too was so natural that St Benedict (6th century) had to forbid it lest the private devotion of a monk paying a visit to the oratory should disturb another with the same intention. But we are a different sort of people, and have long lost that tradition. It seems however that the time has come for us to recover this deep mutual understanding that comes from a genuine sharing in prayer. Certainly it is a channel through which may be remedied those failings in charity of which we have spoken, failings which are accepted too easily because they are not overt sins, and which lead us to take the absence of fulfilment as normal. When it is our turn to be written about, may not the history of spirituality show us as being at the end of a long period in which prayer was understood to be either personal and solitary, or public and formal, and excluded a way in which the community praises God in sentiments that are at once personal, free and joyous? Shared prayer – especially when orientated to a new infusion of the Holy Spirit – may well be the key to collective advance in the love of the brotherhood. Nor will it be a something new but something recovered.

Often there are persons in religious houses who are advanced in prayer. Years of constancy and practice had brought their reward. They are in some stage of the comtemplative life. Have such persons anything to gain by attending a charismatic prayer-meeting? They may well feel, even if they would be slow to say so, that their prayer already reaches a higher level and a deeper intimacy than can be possible in group-prayer. Probably the semi-verbal prayer methods of the group will not attract such persons, nor seem relevant to their further progress.

Three points are worth making here. Firstly, that the style of a prayer meeting, which is affected by the frequency of prayers uttered aloud, is something that should be varied to suit the participants. A religious or monastic group might well want to be more silent than a lay one. The concept of a largely silent sharing is by no means impossible. But it should not be forgotten that in praying out loud we admit others to a sharing in the grace we receive, and unquestionably there are graces received for that end, that is, for the benefit of others. To pray then also on a lower level than one might do alone may be a worthwhile thing on account of the help given to others.

Secondly, it is also possible that through the prayer-meeting God may give *additional* graces to those he gives in private prayer. What emerges through the prayer-meeting is a sense of grace received through the being together, through learning thus to be 'of one heart and one soul', through the stronger perception of the vitality of the Mystical Body of Christ. Even to persons of deep prayer habits one would suggest that there is for them in the prayer meeting a new and valuable experience – to meet the Lord *in others,* to become fruitful for him in others, and to enjoy and praise him in his wonderful work as it takes place in others. It can be that they have much to give in this way – and also that he has *something more* to give them.

Hence (thirdly) they may receive in this way additional gifts, helping them to serve others more effectively. The task of helping others often calls for a mixture of discernment, tact and courage, plus the effective working of the Holy Spirit in the hearts of both helper and helped. As we have said elsewhere the gifts by which we are enabled to help others are called 'service gifts'; they are sometimes like new talents, and sometimes are the same talents but improved and strengthened by the divine touch. Always and everywhere there are needs that call for the compassion and sympathy of those who have it in their power to alleviate them. Everywhere there are the needs of moral, physical and psychological healing. A lively charity bids us do what we can for our suffering neighbour: but supposing that through God's free gift we can do *more,* have we not a duty to dispose ourselves for that gift? Is it right to be contented with poorer resources if God is ready to give richer ones?

Spiritual people will not be unaware of the dangers that special gifts bring with them; nor of the danger of wanting for a too personal reason to be gifted in some special way. But it is not enough to add up the dangers and draw a neat line under the sum. The greater law is charity. And this surely is what the Spirit of God is saying to the Churches in so many fields today. The greater law is to accept every expansion of our personality that God may want to give us in order that we may contribute to the coming of his Kingdom on earth by witnessing to his presence as fully as he wills. The parable about the talents is relevant to us, if God indicates his readiness to meet the needs of our world today by giving us more gifts, more talents in the divine sense, and saying 'Use all this to the maximum for my glory!'

It sometimes happens in monasteries and convents that with the permission of the superior, a small group meets to pray together, and that for whatever reasons, there is no noticeable growth. Other persons, whether members of the community or lay persons, may join them occasionally, but over a long period there is no growth in numbers. And further, the group are not conscious of receiving any particular gifts. Apparently they have added a period of voluntary prayer together to the normal schedule, but nothing special happens. They may even get a bit tired of hearing one another pray. There can be a feeling of discouragement:

'The Holy Spirit is not for us' would be a crude way of expressing it. What of this situation?

1.   The members of the group may do well to check up on their readiness to receive the Spirit. Readiness here does not mean worthiness for we shall never find ourselves worthy. But there are three fundamental dispositions on which we might do well to reflect. Have we purged our souls as well as we can of any unforgivingness that may lurk in them? Secondly, have we an ardent desire for the infusion of the Holy Spirit? This is not the same thing as hoping to receive his gifts. It is the Giver of whose presence we have the primary need. He is always present in the sanctified soul, but it is the unsatisfied desire that he may make his presence felt that is a sign that he will come afresh; because the desire is already from him. And thirdly is there a willingness to surrender to the One who is entreated to come? We may do well to check on these dispositions.

2.   A small group of its own may be misled by expecting things about which it has read or heard, and which appeal to it, and so lose sight of what the Holy Spirit is actually saying to them. He may be at work in them, quietly, like a 'gentle breeze', yet effectively; but because something else is expected, something actually much less radical, the work of the Spirit is not perceived; and this means that co-operation with him will be only partial. Thus renewal is slowed down.

3.   A small group which is beginning may be a bit timid about ministering to one another. It may be wise in such a case to invite some more experienced person to visit them and lead a meeting. They should remember that to pray with or over another is not an exclusive hierarchical privilege; it is an act of practical love. It also grows as a gift, and the great thing is to begin simply with trust in God.

4.   Finally, the most important thing of all may be just to persevere, trusting in the Lord's saying: 'Whoever comes to me I shall not turn him away' (John 6.37, J.B.). To hearts that are open and that long for him, sooner or later will be granted their desire. It is not of course enough to attend a

77

group casually and occasionally; to do this hardly amounts to seeking the infusion of the Spirit with perseverance and sincerity. It is known that some are called to entreat his infusion for quite a long time before they receive it; others he invades almost unasked; but the dabbler falls into neither category.

Religious institutes very properly set a high store on the possession of peace in their midst, and this causes them to worry lest the spirit of renewal proves in effect a spirit of disturbance; yet this is not the real cause for fear. The real causes for fear are not what the Spirit may have to say to us, but rather lest he should have nothing to say to us; or that we should have no ears of what he has to say.

4 The Charismatic Prayer Meeting

The number of charismatic prayer-groups in this country is very large★ and is growing continuously. Hence it may happen that a number of persons decide that they want to set up a charismatic group. Often the beginnings of a group are small: a few persons feel the desire to come together to pray; they have heard that wonderful things happen in the Charismatic Movement; or they have taken part in some meetings elsewhere, and wish to set up a similar group in the hope that the same results may follow in their own parish or institute. How should they set about it?

If it is at all possible they will do well to invite some one of experience to visit them seven weeks running to give them a *seminar* or course of instruction. If this is not possible, then to read books covering the essential themes is the next best thing. It will not be enough just to copy what they have seen others doing; that could be a well-intentioned but lifeless procedure. They need them to be clear about what they are aiming at and to understand how their particular style of meeting will help towards this end. They should not be surprised if their fellow-worshippers are not over sympathetic to their enterprise. For piety is nearly always highly conservative in tone, and they are self-confessed seekers on a path of discovery. Frequently then they cannot expect much approval to begin with.

It will be the more necessary then for them to have a clear idea of what they are about. This indeed they learn as they proceed but a few preliminary ideas are also useful.

★The official list of Catholic sponsored groups in England lists 450 circles, with 27 for Wales (June 1978). There are undoubtedly many more.

1.   The first object of their meeting will be quite simply to praise God. Is not that what every Church service is about? It is; and no one can raise any objection to their meeting together to praise God, even if some wonder why they want something additional to and other than the normally recognised worship. In fact there is already a distinction to be made. For the charismatic group meets in order to *learn* to praise God; and to learn this largely of God himself. As in all worship they will have a leader (or leaders) in their prayers, and there will be reading and exposition, yet they come together knowing that they have a lot more to learn about the inwardness of praising God, and that of this 'lot more', God is the real teacher.

We may explain this a bit further thus:-

To praise God is the end for which God made every creature.

Thus the innate instinct leading us to praise God is the result of the fact that we have received from him a participation in his own blissful existence. Existence is a participation of God's existence; God's existence is total joy. Hence our nature has a need to cry out its acknowledgement of this truth.

To praise God is to assert it, and as far as we can, to assert it more and more resoundingly. 'I AM' cries the creature 'because YOU made me; and You are all goodness and happiness, in which through your gifts to me of existence I share.'

And our existence is of a very special kind, since we are made in his image and likeness, in the image and likeness of God who is all beneficence and joy.

To praise God is to assert this relationship. We have to learn to assert it in all its fullness. It calls for total submission and reverence; it contains the pledge of total fulfilment and joy.

So praising God, the creature fulfils itself, declares God's goodness and expects to be initiated into this reality, through accepting from him a spark of his joy.

Now this has to be learnt, experientially. It concerns us at every level. It calls for the use of the mind's understanding; it calls for the engagement of the affections; it invites also the co-operation of the body, by voice and by symbolic action. It is the business of every level of the human personality; and opens the road to human fulfilment.

It is a fact that while every congregation assembles in its place of worship to praise God and does praise God there, there is little opportunity, as a rule, for its acquiring this sense of reaching God in a prayer that exults in the sharing of his joyous existence. For to know God intellectually, even to know, by faith, that we ought to exult in *sharing existence* with God is not the same thing as learning through experience, in which God rather than man is the teacher, to exult in the sharing of his existence; knowledge about joy is not the same thing as joy itself. It is like the menu pasted up inside the window of the restaurant. Joy in God has to be learnt through the act of praising him. To know this is to know also that we have to do our best to lay ourselves open to his action as we pray. For our act of praise is not a one-sided procedure, but an action in which God shows his good pleasure by communicating joy in himself to those who praise him. Thus the prayer of praise is in itself a petition in the larger sense. For this reason the prayer-meeting is tuitional; it opens by calling on Jesus to be present among those gathered in his name, and to send his Holy Spirit, the only one who can actually impart joy among them. He uses instruments, but essentially he is the tutor.

2. The realisation that Jesus is Lord.

The learning of the content of the simple affirmation "Jesus is Lord" is also in itself a process. 'No one', said St Paul, 'can say "Jesus is Lord" unless he is under the influence of the Holy Spirit' (I Cor. 12.3, J.B.). This means, at the least, that no one can make the act of faith implied in the words 'Jesus is Lord' without the grace to do so. But the statement 'Jesus is Lord' contains depths to which we can only be introduced by the Holy Spirit. It calls for a process

81

by which we come to *realise* that through Christ God reunites all his universe to himself; God the Son is for ever man that being man he may draw us to himself at our human level. For it is indeed all Christ's Kingdom in which as Lord he listens attentively to his brothers and sisters, and will work ceaselessly in each of them; there is no situation in his kingdom which is not his business, or about which he can do nothing. The profounder our submission, the more intense his activity in and through us. If on our side we seek from him liberation, by the process of faith, we also set him free to work in his kingdom. As then the members of the group gather weekly for their prayer, this process should reach deeper levels as they learn to recognise Christ and his power in the here and now.

3. It is to the Third Person of the Blessed Trinity that we attribute the work of our interior renewal. And we think of him, using the scriptural formula, as being sent by Jesus. The nature of the grace of renewal has already been explained (pp. 9–14). It is then to obtain this grace that the meeting is specifically orientated, and to obtain the gifts of the Spirit that come with it. It prays earnestly for the coming of the Holy Spirit upon itself collectively, and on its members individually; and it prays expectantly. It senses this effusion of the Spirit on itself as a group by certain signs, as when its prayer develops a collective harmony, when the same spiritual desires or thoughts arise simultaneously in different persons, when it perceives that its prayers are answered by God with what seems a new generosity, when confidence grows and joy with it, and the promises of the Saviour are as real as if he stood there pronouncing them anew.

The members of the group find themselves undergoing similar but not identical processes. There is the penetration of repentance (*metanoia*), coming to each as it applies to his own past life. Without this renewal will not have much depth, may even prove superficial and transient. There is the mutual love that grows between the members as they come to perceive that they are channels of grace to one another.

82

There is in all a sense of the growth of the love of the Lord Jesus in their hearts, and a sense that this growth is definitely not their own work and could not be; and there is wonder too as they perceive the same thing in others.

Then too there are the gifts by which the Holy Spirit makes plain his presence. These vary in abundance; it is said that their profuseness is related to the way in which the group performs its basic task of praising God, more being received where more ardent praise has been given. There is a correspondence too between the nature of the gifts given and the spiritual needs of the group. The Holy Spirit does not grant gifts for which there will be no use, either because they would not correspond to the tasks that the group members have to perform, or because individuals are not ready or willing to accept the responsibility that such gifts bring.

There is something here that must make us reflect, for in our human affairs the quality of responsibility is of the highest significance, almost to the point of fixing the social value of an individual. But is it always to the most humanly suitable that these spiritual gifts are given? Our Lord said: 'I thank you, Father, for that you have hidden these things from the wise and prudent, and revealed them to little ones' (Luke 10.21, Douai). Is that because the 'little ones' find it easier to accept their own ignorance of the divine? A confession of ignorance, even of culpable ignorance, may be the required starting line in this kind of race.

It has been said (p. 11) that one of the elements in the grace of renewal is joy. It does not however always come at once, as certain books might seem to imply. Experience however, shows that, for whatever reasons, some persons have a long road to travel before they reach it. It may be because they have unconsciously (or even deliberately) shut out joy from their hearts for many years; or perhaps through no fault of their own, but from the circumstances of their lives, they have never known much of human joy. Whatever the cause they present themselves as spiritually joyless persons, walled in by their years of distress; as the group proceeds to show itself more joyful, they who are untouched by this may feel that they are being left behind. But they do not have to fear. They will be changed all right. The Lord has a pick-axe, and in time the wall will come down. Maybe the delay is due to their own inability to co-operate more closely; they should give therefore all the co-operation of faith and confidence that they can; and if they become aware of any unforgiveness in their hearts they must react against it.

That aspect of renewal, which leads to improvement in the personalities of the members of the group, will not in itself bring down disapproval from their neighbours and fellow-worshippers. Indeed our neighbours may think that the process (however it works) ought to be going faster, and they may in fact expect too soon to see the fruits of an interior growth, which is only just beginning to assert itself. There is however another aim of the group, which can run into a lot of misunderstanding. For the third orientation of the group is towards the manifestation of Christ's power.

Everyone (or nearly everyone) is aware and accepts that in his life Our Lord gave ample manifestations of his power. A very large part of the Gospels is devoted to accounts of this. Our Lord used his power not only that we might believe in him; he used it that we might understand his Father's love; he used it because, being who he was, he felt true compassion when faced with human needs of healing. He could not claim to be our Saviour and healer merely in the abstract: he was under an inner necessity to let his power come into use at the instance of his compassion.

The Gospels tell us also, that the Apostles were sent out by him to preach in his name with the aid of miracles (Matt. 10.1; Luke 9.1). Without these powers they would not have had much success.

Unto our own times a double tradition of wonder-working has continued in the Church, and in varying degrees received recognition. Thus miracles of healing have been sought at special shrines; and various wonder-working powers have been accredited to certain persons of recognised holiness. Doubtful legends have certainly accumulated round certain personalities, and shrines have not always been free of superstitious practices. But with these reservations it is certainly true that the tradition that Christ continues to manifest his power both directly and through the prayers of his saints, has never disappeared from the Church.

Today it is claimed here and there and everywhere, and not in one denomination only, that in our highly technological materialistic rationalising age, the Lord manifests his presence in power. This should be encouraging for all believers, but in fact seems to strain the belief of some of them, as it is beyond the ordinary expectations of their faith. For some persons, indeed, it is a shock, and in a narrower sense, shocking, when ordinary persons of their acquaintance claim that the Lord does wonderful things through their prayers, or that he has done wonderful things for them. Moreover to ask for such things, and to really expect them seems over bold.

Tradition has a lot to do with our attitudes. It is accepted as all right for a group of children to pray for fine weather; and there is no shock if the weather turns out to be fine (perhaps because in this country it *might* have turned out fine anyway). It is not the same thing at all if a prayer-group prays that some sick person may receive her health, and lays hands on her and invokes the power of the Lord; that will upset some people and be thought of as 'going too far'. After all, if the person recovers, an alternative explanation may not be so easy to find. We are unwilling to call out aloud our desires for the Lord to manifest his power; though tradition permits it to be done in private prayer or (not too expressively) in public worship. Yet the charismatic group aims also at this. An increased awareness that the Lord is always at work, manifesting his loving care in the preservation of his children in the ordinary business of their lives, makes it more natural for them to pray in a situation of greater need, without *feeling* that this is unwarranted or asking too much. The assumption behind the prayer is that Christ wants us so to pray in our needs, and will react to faith according to his promises. It is not that he is more beneficent to some than to others, but that faith releases his power. Nor is it necessary to think in terms of asking 'miracles'; but rather that all our universe is totally subject to Christ its Lord, who himself Man as well as God has complete authority and power to do in it as he wills. It is natural then for him to exercise his authority and manifest his power, on behalf of his brothers and sisters. Our part is to ask for this in humility, but also with confidence. This is why it is not felt to be presumptuous to ask for the healing of bodies or the lifting of psychological traumata or the solution of difficult situations.

And there is constant confirmation of the divine promises to answer prayer. The Lord still confirms the word by the signs that accompany it (Mark 16.20). It is not that every petition is answered in the form it is asked for; but the number of signs by which the Lord confirms his hearing of our prayers is greatly increased. He remains from our point of view unpredictable; that is to say, we often do not know with any certainty what he will find best; we do know that somehow our prayer in faith and our expectancy does play a part in releasing his compassionate power. We have to learn to live in this relationship with him in which we confidently ask him to use his power, accept it joyfully when this is evident (this part is not difficult), and remain not less sure of his compassion and attention, when the result of our prayers is not evident to us.

If we are really surprised when our prayers are answered, and not at all surprised when nothing seems to happen, that implies that our faith is not very expectant. There is a definite correlation, as we said before, between the manifestation of divine power and the humble expectancy of faith (Mark 6.5).

In general then, a third aim of the group is to become an instrument through which the divine authority and compassion of Christ may flow freely . . . to become like the branch of a tree called on to bear all kinds of fruit for its Master. We may also compare it to a channel or a pipe for all kinds of graces. Then we realise that it has to be open, unblocked, a free passage-way; and it also has to be pure. These responsibilities lie on it.

A group that understands clearly these three aims, and that they are likely to come about progressively over a period of time, and in the order in which they have been set out, will know that its meetings are not a place where 'happenings' are sought for their own sake. They are in context only in the work of spreading the extent and deepening the power of Christ's kingdom.

Neither has the organizing of a charismatic meeting anything in common with promoting a club for lonely hearts, or stimulating a happy party atmosphere.

Least of all are the group called to become an élite, treasuring secrets and acquiring powers unknown to the ordinary Christian. All that they learn is knowledge available to and desirable in the ordinary Christian; the joyousness that they find in their prayer is for all who desire it. *He that hath ears to hear let him hear. He that is thirsty let him come and drink.*

*****

The group will need a leader. There are advantages if he is also their priest; but we have to reckon with – to welcome indeed – that God is raising up lay leaders in his Church and endowing them with the necessary gifts.

The leader of a weekly meeting however is not necessarily the same as the overall leader of the group. Indeed there is a lot to be said for variety in the conduct of the meetings, provided that adequate talent is available, and provided also that the general shape and outline of the proceedings has already been determined.

Apart from the qualities normally implied in the word,

the leader of a prayer group should have two specific qualities. The first is simply that of having acquired some experience in what it is about and how this type of prayer-meeting functions. Secondly, he or she, should be a person of sensitivity. In ordinary affairs dictators are undesirable, and spiritual dictators are worse. Prayer is a very intimate thing, and one of the characteristics of the prayer-meeting is that out of so many individual intimacies with God it builds a new communal intimacy that does not destroy but brings more fruit to the individual ones. This is a gradual process, as various members of the group grow – at their own speeds – in liberation from their inhibitions and in their capacity to glorify God. (What sounds so simple in the persons of the Gospel, 'who followed him along the road, glorifying God', seems to take quite a bit of learning today.) To help this process forward is a delicate task, calling for a sensitivity in the leader to the unspoken needs of others. He has to be conscious of what others are wanting or perhaps finding unwanted in the course of the meetings, and to be alert to the direction in which the Spirit seems to be calling the minds of the group. This can well present human problems, since the proficiency of the group to pray as a united body cannot be taken for granted. It is something learnt gradually; to begin with some may be unable to contribute at all, some may be temperamentally inclined to contribute too much, some to go off at a tangent without reference to the general stream of the prayer. Proficiency in this kind of prayer is something that comes to a group by degrees, and does not exclude a normal process of learning. And there are likely to be newcomers who need special help in understanding the aims and procedures; for these indeed, as already said, a seminar is really the best procedure.

For these reasons it is advisable for any group of a certain size – say a dozen or more – to have a CORE group as well as a leader. The CORE group has additional meetings of which the general scope is to make things flow smoothly and to promote the progress of the whole group.

They will tackle problems that may arise: What is to be done if a difficult neurotic arrives and is found to be disturbing? What if some one appears to evince a gift of prophecy; is it genuine? Did the last meeting run smoothly, or was there a kind of bumpiness in the proceedings, due to members failing to listen to one another and going off at a tangent? Since the group consists of ordinary persons, as yet inexperienced in a kind of prayer that is simultaneously collective, loosely organized and spontaneous, there are likely to be problems.

Sometimes too the CORE group has to consider suggestions for further progress, questions concerning special expeditions, or larger reunions, or visiting the sick or the ministry of healing.

Very often prayer is an important part of *their* meeting also. For example, there is some problem, and some difference of opinion; it is not just thrashed out in argument; all pray silently for a while that the right answer may be found. Afterwards discussion is found to go much easier. Sometimes the CORE groups spends most of its time in silent prayer. At an ordinary meeting it is not always possible to give lengthy stretches to silent prayer since this would not suit everybody. Yet for some this may be what they need most.

Another function that the CORE group fulfils is that of providing 'feed-back' for the leader: from it he can learn the reactions of group-members or visitors to this or that procedure or to some particular teaching session. Again the group may be of help in the choice of different persons to lead individual meetings. In general it shares the responsibilities of its leader, and its meetings serve for the evaluation of what happens at the larger meeting.

It is essential that the CORE group consists of responsible people. It is not enough to talk in tongues, or to find that one really enjoys attendance at the prayer meeting. Each member of the CORE group must feel true love, and therefore care for the members of the whole group, and be concerned for them. Large groups will usually contain some persons who attend fairly frequently because they like it, but do not develop any deep commitment; and others who are there compulsively because of some need; and some who come steadily, profit unquestionably, but do not apparently contribute much – although they may actually be making an unseen contribution. But the member of the CORE group accepts the responsibility to give all that he can in whatever ways correspond to his personal talents or the gifts that have been given him.

Let us turn now to the prayer-meeting itself. It is made up of different elements. In fact, as in the Divine Office, there are three essential strands – the prayer of praise, the prayer of petition, and listening to the divine word. But they have far more varied forms than in liturgical worship. Thus we may distinguish:

In the prayer of praise:-

Hymn singing
Individual spontaneous prayer
Collective praise

In the prayer of petition:-

Intercessions
'Baptism in the Spirit'
Prayer for healings
Prayer over one another ('Ministering' to one another).

Listening to the divine word:-

Reading and Exposition of Scripture
Messages given in tongues and interpreted
Prophecy
Periods of silence

Not all these elements will be necessarily be found at any one meeting; and it is possible to add one or two other elements also; the giving of testimony, announcements, discussion. There is a great variety in the way in which meetings are conducted. The time available, the customs of the group, its size, its natural talents, its supernatural gifts, all affect the proceedings. It is the business of the leader to indicate when to pass from one element to another. With these preliminaries, it may be useful to give a general description of a meeting. We shall cover all that is likely to be found at a full-length meeting of (say) two hours, or over a series of shorter meetings.

1. Normally the meeting will open with prayer uttered in praise of God. This may take the form of singing a psalm or hymn; or it may be done through the recitation by one of a psalm of praise. Frequently the leader utters an extempore prayer to open the meeting. Occasionally meetings open with a simultaneous murmur of prayer from all present: this is known as 'the word of prayer' (sometimes this is done later).

It should be noted that while some form of praise, it matters not which, is the usual way of opening, the *whole* meeting has for its purpose the praise of God. It is not just a preliminary item.

2. Often at an early stage the meeting will fall into silence. This is not the silence of emptiness, nor an interval between activities, but a very positive moment in which through silent prayer, all lay themselves open to God's grace. It is a time when the Spirit of God is active in hearts, promoting love, stirring repentance, giving new light or new courage, as the case may be. It is important that there should be an attitude of submission and surrender to him who is invited.

This silence is likely to be interrupted by utterances of prayer from individuals as they feel prompted. For some persons there may be a real difficulty about so praying aloud, especially if the group is a large one. This may well disappear

91

with time, but there is the danger of some saying too much and others too little. In general it is desirable that each member should contribute, since thereby comes liberation of spirit, and thereby the shackles of modern conventions are overcome. There are however other forms of contribution, such as reading from the Scripture. The belief in the background to this style of prayer is that our relationship with God is not *only* a private matter, to be kept in a cupboard well out of sight, even as God's redemption of man was not just a private matter but of significance to human society as such, and something that we should share and rejoice over together. That is what we find in Sacred Scripture, both in the Old Testament and the New; no one would deny it in theory, but in effect we may have a state of affairs in which conventions permit the response of joy to show itself only in words already fixed by hymns or already composed prayers.

It should be noted by those who contribute to the build-up of this united but spontaneous prayer, that they are endeavouring to pray as one body. They should therefore be alert to the emergence of a theme. This is a moment in which it is hoped that the Holy Spirit will lead the group in one direction. When this is so, similar but different and personal thoughts and aspirations arise in each, and when they are uttered, it is found that there arises a common meditation on some aspect of the divine goodness or our redemption. This implies that each listens to what the other says, joining with it and carrying the theme forward; at times however when some one has made a powerful utterance with thoughts that bespeak interior inspiration, the appropriate reponse is silence, while the content is taken in. It cannot be said that a theme always emerges clearly; in this respect meetings vary a good deal. The reading of Scripture early on in the meeting may help towards it. In any case the intention of praying unitedly is always to be borne in mind. If problems arise, it will be the business of the CORE group to consider them; if the group is a small one it may be advisable to hold an occasional discussion to make sure that all are satisfied about this important part of their prayer.

3. As we have said intercessions for specific intentions come under a different heading. We are all familiar with the prayer of petition, the more so since the introduction of Bidding Prayers into our liturgy. Petitions are not only a necessary part of our prayer inasmuch as there are always things we stand in need of for ourselves, but they have also the valuable function of turning the prayer of the meeting in an outward direction. Most people have someone in their life about whom they have cause for anxiety, and for whom they are glad to have an opportunity to obtain prayers. There are also, and this is of considerable significance, the wider issues. The news of the day often gives matter for prayer. There are aspects of the life of the Church which should not be forgotten; prayer for the Bishop, the parish priest; prayer for those suffering behind the Iron Curtain, or in disturbed countries in Africa or S. America; prayer for missionaries, for local needs, for vocations to the priesthood or religious life; prayers for individual sufferers whether in mind or in body. There is no end to the potential list.

In this particular kind of prayer it is certainly desirable that all should make their intentions known, but not all are equally able to voice a prayer. A way of facilitating the prayer of intercession is to divide a larger group into smaller ones. The small groups separate into huddles; in each huddle one who is more proficient helps the others as far as may be necessary, but not more, to declare their intention, and then the group pauses to pray for it, before passing on to the next person. The leader of the whole meeting allows an adequate space of time, so that all have a chance to have their intentions prayed for, and then brings the complete meeting together again for whatever comes next.

4. An important element in most meetings is the reading of a passage of Scripture; a teaching may then be based on it. In this way members of the group are instructed directly from Scripture, on how to translate Christ's teaching into

their daily lives, on what the Holy Spirit may be saying to them about their lives, the graces they should hope for, the significance of being a member of Christ's Mystical Body, what the gifts of the Holy Spirit are, etc.

Thus the Scriptures are studied anew, and in fact 'opened' to some who have not hitherto studied them with any consistency. The aim is not precisely exegetic (a study of literal meaning), but the revelation of spiritual content and its relevance to ourselves. A knowledge of exegesis however is valuable; among other advantages it prevents the making of highly personal interpretations of phrases or sentences, out of context with the author's meaning.

Alternatively a reading from Scripture may be followed by the silence of meditation.

5. A feature which seems to be special to the charismatic meeting is the giving of testimonies. These are not properly speaking, a form of prayer, nor are they a part of every meeting. A testimony occurs when some one feels called on to bear witness to the work of the Lord in his life – or it may be that he bears personal witness to the work of the Lord in the life of another. Such testimonies can be very impressive, as when some one feels called on to make known a deeply felt call of grace or a sense of contrition embracing wide areas of his life. This can be an operation difficult for the speaker and intensely moving for others. It can result in an extraordinary sense of liberation from past bonds whether of sin or indifference or inhibition. A profound testimony to a deep change in personality is of course comparatively rare. After all it is an interior miracle.

It is this element especially which gives rise to the image that charismatic meetings are occasions for unbridled hysteria, in which powerful preachers work on simple-minded folk until they pass into an emotional state in which with cries and sobs they denounce themselves, and declare themselves saved. No doubt an investigator setting out in search of such phenomena can find them without much difficulty; reference has been made in Chapter I to the bad image of

94

Pentecostals. But to the ordinary frequenter of charismatic meetings such narrations are like a wild caricature of what happens. The Catholic practice of individual confessions has also suffered from the caricatures of those who disapproved of it. Nor is public confession necessarily the product of hysteria. In the early Church it was the normal procedure in the sacrament of penance. It had – and has – the advantage that the social consequences of sin were recognised and, equally, the social consequences of repentance.

Such profound testimonies, however, are, in the nature of the case, rather rare. Most of the time the testimonies are very simple relations, even trivial ones, of how the speaker recognized the finger of God in some event in his own life. He may want to give thanks to God for some new happiness in his life, for a healing, for the deliverance from a phobia, for a remarkable answer to prayer, or even for something that happened to another. Repentance is not the only theme: God's guidance, God's protection, prayers answered, new openings spiritual, social or religious, whatever speaks of God manifesting himself in our affairs may be the subject of a testimony.

6. Sometimes there has to be a time in a meeting similar to the one in Church worship in which 'notices' are given out. These obviously concern anything exceptional that may be forthcoming, anything that has to be organized, or it may be visiting the sick, etc. This is a time when questions can be asked.

Nor are discussions unknown, though they do not belong as a prayer item. Small groups that have no other opportunity to come together outside their regular meeting may find it profitable to open up to one another in a frank interchange of views from time to time.

7. One of the items which a CORE group may have to consider is the exercise of the gift of prophecy. By no means every group contains a member gifted with prophecy; it is a precious gift by which the Lord manifests his presence, and hence prophets rightly enjoy esteem. In spite of popular

usage the word in itself does not imply foretelling; it means simply the capacity to serve as a channel for a message from God. But there is bound to arise the question: Is the person who speaks in prophecy, that is in the person of God, doing so genuinely or not? There are three possibilities: true prophecy, false prophecy (due to fraud or even evil inspiration) and non-prophecy or well-meant self-delusion. The Old Testament knew two tests of prophecy: whether what was foretold turned out to be true, and whether what was said was in accord with the recognized moral and spiritual teaching of Yahweh. Since however charismatic prophets frequently do not foretell anything, they cannot be judged by that criterion, nor does the other type of test necessarily yield an answer. Yet discernment and acceptance or rejection there has to be. The known personal character of the person who seems to be so gifted is the first criterion. A prophet in whom the gift is coming into force often has an internal struggle as he feels he should use it, makes an utterance and yet is not sure of what his impulse means. As with certain other gifts however it grows in power. Sometimes it seems it has to grow in purity, inasmuch as the rendering of a divine message without any personal admixture does not always come at once.

If there is uncertainty the CORE group may have to judge. Sometimes alas! there is not much uncertainty, and it can be clear that a good person is deluding himself with the notion that he is prophesying, whereas in fact he is uttering pious words of his own composition. Cases have been known where the motive is less worthy: some misguided person seeks to gain prestige for himself by setting up as a prophet. There must then be *discernment,* and this too is a special gift of the Spirit which is expected by charismatics, and may well be fairly generally dispersed among the members of the group. Credulity is no virtue, but suspiciousness is not equivalent to discernment which implies a capacity to make a positive judgment as well as a negative one. Priests, whether by virtue of their ordination or their practical experience of humanity in its religious behaviour, seem to have a fairly sure gift for distinguishing the fraudulent. They may need however to grow in the more positive capacity of discerning when the Spirit is really present.

In some cases the prophetic gift declares itself strongly, compulsively even. In others it is at first like the mere glimmer of a low-powered electric light bulb; but from this small beginning it grows into a powerful light.

There is no precise time in a meeting for a manifestation of prophecy: a prophet often speaks out of a period of silence. If the message is a striking one, it will be followed by a period of silence.

8.   The gift of tongues is not infrequently received during a meeting, and in particular in connection with the prayer for the effusion of the Spirit. It is however not often used in a way that would interrupt the normal procedure of the meeting, unless through it there appears to be a message for the assembly; and in that case, the correlative gift, that of interpretation will be called for. Quite common however is the practice of singing in tongues; this means that all so gifted sing together using their respective tongues, following their own melody, but forming a mysterious harmony.

This is not the place to enter on a discussion of why charismatics today should speak in tongues, nor why indeed the Apostles and first Christians should have done so, nor what is the precise psychological explanation.* Suffice it to say that charismatics accept the gift joyfully, but, knowing its limitations, use it rather sparingly at their meetings.

9.   If one gathers together a dozen ordinary people, it would be surprising if it turned out that no one among them had a need for healing. Some one will have a limp, another will be a bit deaf, and, for sure, there will be invisible aches and pains distributed among them. Equally surely there will be in some of them the marks of the sorrows, even the

*It is dealt with at great length in Killian McDonnell's: *Charismatic Renewal and the Churches* (Seabury Press, 1975). Every aspect seems to be dealt with in his final assessment in 28 points (pp. 152–6).

tragedies, that have marked their lives. The proportion of wounded people is high.

In a larger gathering the probability of the meeting containing more extreme cases will be greater. It may well include the decidedly neurotic, persons with grave moral problems, persons in some way afflicted by evil powers. . . . This is humanity as we know it.

Nor was it any different in the beginning. The New Testament writers leave us in no doubt that they were perfectly aware that they were still dealing with wounded humanity, and that their converts had known much of sin and would still feel the same temptations. Paul wrote many warnings about the danger of falling back into grave sins. For example 'Let us give up all the things we prefer to do under cover of the dark . . . no drunken orgies, no promiscuity, no licentiousness' (Rom. 13.12–13, J.B.). And Peter tells his readers: 'None of you should ever deserve to suffer for being a murderer, a thief, a criminal or an informer' (I Peter 4.15, J.B.). Evidently the Church was recruited from all kinds of men*.

If there were these spiritual wounds, there were physical and psychological ones also. Nothing has changed in these circumstances, unless it be that for physical and psychological sicknesses far more skilful treatment by natural means is now available. However, there remains and will always remain a great gap between the availability of such natural means, and indeed their power, and our needs.

If follows then that those who are gathered together in the name of Jesus, and are encouraged by his promises and the teaching and examples in holy Scripture, will turn to him for the healing of their ills. Hence the praying of a group over a single person for some specific need is a common sight at charismatic meetings. It is not regarded as an alternative to medicine or psychiatry. For these may be going on

---

*cf. Gal. 5.19–20 for a long list of grave sins, and II Cor. 12.21, for a plain statement that he is talking about present temptations.

simultaneously. Prayer may help them in responding to such remedial work; or it may prove the one remedy that is effective, since it goes beyond what can be reasonably hoped for by natural means.

Nor does the prayer of a group over one person, or of one person over another imply that something is amiss. For we always need more of God's grace, desire more of his gifts and stand at the beginning of the experience of his love. To some persons in particular is given a powerful ministry to help others through their prayer; sometimes it is a ministry for physical healing, sometimes for interior (psychological or spiritual) healing, sometimes for both; it seems that physical and psychological healings are not conferred by Our Lord without a definite effect of grace. And it is by this mark that their source is recognized. For other healers there are, and these other healers do not have this effect.

In fact, between praying over a person for an interior grace or a new gift and praying over a person for a healing, the gulf is not necessarily very great. For our needs are really a continuous chain from the purely spiritual through the psychological to the simply physical. But there is a distinction to be made between ordinary healing and prayer for deliverance from evil. The last is a subject of great significance especially for priests, on account of the ministry and powers formally accredited to them. In deliverance from evil the prayer takes the form of a command to the evil power to depart and leave the person free. The effects are often extraordinary.[1]

Prayer for healing is then a common feature at a meeting. It takes time, and is therefore frequently done at the end of the general meeting, by a group, for the person or persons concerned. Through such prayers (though by no means only so) a more or less marked 'ministry of healing' can appear

[1] Fr Jim McManus C.S.S.R. points out that the moral theologians were perfectly familiar with and recommended this practice to priests in general. He cites Noldin and Prummer. *Anointed in the Spirit* (Mayhew-McCrimmon, 1978), p. 57.

99

in one person; that is to say, the person becomes aware through experience that the Lord will make use of him frequently and powerfully for the healing of others. Such persons do not think of themselves as 'healers' for they know that it is the healing power of Jesus that flows through them, and not their own.[2] Very often they do not know themselves whether in fact this will happen, but in some cases they have a sensation by which they know that it is happening.

What perhaps calls for emphasis is this: As a group learns to pray and answers are received, its faith is increased. It grows stronger, more open, and becomes a fitter vehicle for divine power. If one may say so without irreverence a kind of divine compound interest is at work. To him that hath (faith) more is given . . . and the answers to the prayer in faith multiply.

For some groups there may be a difficulty about getting started. The unfamiliarity of the procedure, the sense of being personally non-gifted, shyness, etc, may make beginnings difficult. A group may sometimes call in a person of known experience to get them moving.

There can be a danger in seeking for oneself a special ministry of healing. Should one not fear that one is secretly, unconsciously even, ministering to one's own need of self-importance? Truly that is a question to be asked. Yet how great is the need for an increase in the ministry in the Church today! How much divine power awaits unlocking! How many need to be delivered from evil! Undoubtedly priests and others should be sensitive to signs of a divine invitation, and generous in responding. But it will be an onerous ministry.

The question is sometimes asked: Since the Church has a special sacrament (the Anointing of the Sick) for healing, should not this be the one channel used? Undoubtedly the sacrament is being used much more and more profitably

---

[2] There are also persons who have natural healing powers, however this be explained. The text does not deal with this situation.

than it was, but that is not a reason for rejecting other means. The faithful have always prayed for and found healing in other ways too. They have always gone and still go on pilgrimage; there have always been some persons endowed with healing gifts; the faithful have always made their own supplications in their homes, etc. Christ fulfils his promises in most diverse ways and it is not for us to limit his largesse by failing to make use of any channel that he makes use of.

10.   Finally a word about 'baptism in the Spirit', in so far as it is an element in a prayer meeting. As has been said, essentially this term is a name – not much liked by some and something of a barrier to others – for the grace of renewal of the Christian's life, or a marked deepening of it. The theological aspects have been discussed in Chapter I; here we refer to it as an element in a prayer meeting. It is customary to pray over those who so desire it, usually at the end of a meeting. Outwardly the procedure resembles that of a prayer for healing. A group gathers round the person to be prayed over, lays on hands, and invokes a new coming of the Spirit, and may ask for special gifts as the case may be. The essential petition is always that the new member may be granted the experience of a closer and richer relationship with Jesus Christ.

Such a prayer is not a sacrament, and has not a covenanted or *ex opere operato* effect. Sometimes it takes effect but in a way only perceived by the recipient of the grace; or it may be accompanied by gifts immediately perceivable by others (for example the gift of tongues). If the person over whom the prayer is made is unable to detect any difference in his state afterwards, even after allowing a space of time to elapse, the conclusion must be that the grace of renewal has not taken place. This *can* happen, for example, when a person presents himself to be prayed over but has made no preparation to find out what it really means, or is activated by no deeper motive than curiosity, or is spiritually unprepared to move forward. Or there may be some interior obstacle. The same person may seek the grace of renewal again later, but should look first to see whether there has been some impediment.

Undoubtedly harm has been done by the spreading of the idea that what is being done is the evoking of a marvellous state of spiritual euphoria (a 'summit experience') likely to last about twenty-four hours, or a bit longer. Unfortunately this corresponds more or less to what many think 'baptism in the Spirit' signifies. The fact that many testify to having received such an experience confirms them in their misapprehension. However the distinction between such wonderful experiences received by some and renewal in the Spirit which is the essential element for all has been referred to in Chapter I.

The normal time for asking to be prayed over in this way is when a person (1) has acquired an adequate knowledge of what it is about, that is, what they are asking for, and (2) is as far as possible in a condition of genuine surrender to whatever God may want of them, and of readiness to accept whatever gifts he may give them. It is not unknown for a person to have a strong repugnance to the idea of receiving the gift of tongues; if so, they should come to terms with this first.

In practice this may imply help with personal difficulties from a group member, or instruction through a seminar. Sometimes it calls for a real act of courage – and in such cases the reward is usually proportionate. However when all is said we have to recognize that while we make rules for these things according to our experience of what works best, our rules do not bind the Holy Spirit. He has a way of showing us this, and when he does it is a cause of wonder and delight. The Scriptural prototype of such a happening is the case of Cornelius in Acts 10. Peter had not finished his sermon before the Holy Spirit descended, and behold! there was Cornelius and his household talking in tongues! As Peter wisely said, nothing remained but to accept the fact, and co-operate with it through conferring baptism.

11.   The Eucharist is not normally a part of the charis-

matic prayer meeting; for the most part this is not possible. It may then be well to stress that it is regularly the highlight of a day or half-day of Renewal, or each day of a longer Conference. For in the Eucharist praise and thanksgiving reach their fullest expression, joy and contrition are deepened.